mustsees
Paris

The Louvre and pyramid with the Eiffel Twoer in the distance / © Arnaud Chicurel/hemis.fr

MICHELIN

mustsees Paris

Editorial Director	Cynthia Clayton Ochterbeck
Edited & Produced by	Jonathan P. Gilbert, Azalay Media
Contributing Writer	Heather Stimmler-Hall
Production Manager	Natasha G. George
Cartography	Stephane Anton, John Dear, Thierry Lemasson
Layout	Natasha G. George
Interior Design	Chris Bell, cbdesign
Cover Design	Chris Bell, cbdesign, Natasha G. George

Contact Us

Michelin Travel and Lifestyle North America
One Parkway South
Greenville, SC 29615
USA
travel.lifestyle@us.michelin.com
www.michelintravel.com

Michelin Travel Partner
Hannay House
39 Clarendon Road
Watford, Herts WD17 1JA
UK
✆ 01923 205240
travelpubsales@uk.michelin.com
www.ViaMichelin.com

Special Sales

For information regarding bulk sales,
customized editions and premium sales,
please contact us at:
travel.lifestyle@us.michelin.com
www.michelintravel.com

Michelin Travel Partner

Société par actions simplifiées au capital de 11 288 880 EUR
27 cours de l'Ile Seguin - 92100 Boulogne Billancourt (France)
R.C.S. Nanterre 433 677 721

© Michelin Travel Partner
ISBN 978-2-067197-39-8
Printed: July 2014
Printed and bound in Italy

MIX
Paper from
responsible sources
FSC® C015829

Welcome to Paris

Galerie des Glaces, Château de Versailles

© S. Sauvignier / MICHELIN

Introduction

p 75

© Didier Zylberyng / Pictures Colour Library

La Défense at night   p 78

© Toutenphoton / Fotolia.com

Basilique Saint-Denis   p 108

© Franco Di Meo/Fotolia.com

Arc de Triomphe   p 72

© Mark Kerr / Michelin

Château de Chantilly p 102

© Jose Fuste Raga / age fotostock

Cathédrale Notre-Dame p 74

© Kaos02 / Sime / Photononstop

Musée Marmottan-Monet p 91

© Sylvain Sonnet / hemis.fr

ACTIVITIES

Unmissable activities and entertainment

Try a macaroon, Ladurée p 129

© Murat Koc/iStockphoto

Climb the Eiffel Tower p 72

© Ilpo Musto / Apa Publications

Soak up the atmosphere in Montmartre   p 62

© S. Sauvignier / Michelin

Browse bookstores p 131

© Mark Kerr / Michelin

Relax on a Parisian beach p 119

© Morane / Fotolia.com

STAR ATTRACTIONS

9

STAR ATTRACTIONS

Unmissable historic, cultural, and natural sights

For more than 75 years people have used Michelin stars to take the guesswork out of travel. Our star-rating system helps you make the best decision on where to go, what to do, and what to see.

★★★	Unmissable
★★	Worth a trip
★	Worth a detour
No star	recommended

MUST KNOW

ACTIVITIES

Unmissable
entertainment,
activities, and
restaurants.

Outings

Explore the
 Catacombes *p30*
Get a bird's eye view
 from Notre-Dame *p74*
Soak up the
 atmosphere in
 Montmartre *p62*
Enjoy a trip on a bateau-
 mouche *p112*
Track down the
 Mona Lisa *p82*
Relax on a Parisian
 beach *p119*
Visit the cathedral in
 Chartres *p103*

Kids

Climb the Eiffel
 Tower *p72*
Take in a 360-degree
 movie at La
 Géode *p114*
See a puppet
 show *p117*

Sports

Swim in the Josephine
 Baker pool *p113*
See Paris by bike *p113*
Make a splash at
 Aquaboulevard *p116*

Shopping

Browse bookstores of
 St-Germain *p131*
Windowshop on the
 Champs-Élysées *p129*

Bargain hunt at a
 flea market *p133*
Try a macaroon from
 Ladurée *p129*

Restaurants

Dine at the
 historic Le Procope
 restaurant *p137*
Enjoy breakfast on the
 boul' St-Michel *p32*
Dine at La Coupole
 brasserie *p141*

Nightlife

Enjoy a night at the
 Paris Opéra *p123*
Take in a show at the
 Moulin-Rouge *p65*
Sip a cocktail at Harry's
 New York Bar *p127*

STAR ATTRACTIONS

CALENDAR OF EVENTS

Listed below are some of the city's most popular annual events.

February
Festival mondial du
Cirque de demain
> International Circus Festival
> of Tomorrow
> *(www.cirquedemain.com)*

Salon international
d'agriculture
> Agricultural show, Parc des
> Expositions, Porte de Versailles
> *(www.salon-agriculture.com)*

February–mid-March
Six Nations Rugby
> Stade de France, St-Denis
> *(www.rbs6nations.com)*

April
Paris Marathon
> The long distance road race
> *(www.parismarathon.com)*

End April–mid-May
Foire de Paris
> Paris Trade Fair, the latest
> in products for the home,
> health, and leisure, Parc des
> Expositions, Porte de Versailles
> *(www.foiredeparis.fr)*

End May–early June
French Open Tennis
> Roland Garros Stadium
> *(www. rolandgarros.com)*

May–July
Paris Jazz Festival
> Parc floral de Vincennes,
> free concerts Sat and
> Sun afternoons
> *(www.parisjazzfestival.fr)*

June
Fête de la Musique
> Music concerts at indoor
> and outdoor venues throughout
> the capital and on the streets
> *(Jun 21)*

Paris Grand Prix
> Horse racing at the Hippodrome
> de Longchamp *(last Sun in Jun;
> www.france-galop.com)*

July
La Fête Nationale (Bastille Day)
> **Celebrations throughout the
> city including:**
> Dancing—firemen's balls in
> fire stations across Paris *(Jul 13)*
> Military parade on the
> Champs-Élysées *(Jul 14)*
> Fireworks display at the
> Trocadéro *(Jul 14)*

Tour de France
> Final stage of the grueling cycle
> race on the Champs-Élysées,
> consisting of 8 laps of the
> famous avenue *(www.letour.fr)*

Allons enfants de la Patrie!

Also known as le Quatorze Juillet (the Fourteenth of July), Bastille
Day festivities normally kick off on the evening of July 13 when the
traditional firemen's balls *(bals des pompiers)* are held at stations
across the city. On July 14 a grand military parade marches down the
Champs-Élysées from the Arc de Triomphe, and in the evening a party
mood reigns supreme as fireworks light up the night sky.

MUST KNOW

Mid-July–mid-August

Paris quartier d'été

Summer arts festival at venues around the city—jazz, theater, music, circus, film, and dance *(www.quartierdete.com)*

Paris Plage

The banks of the Seine are transformed into a car-free beach zone with parasols, sunloungers, palm trees, and recreation areas *(see For Kids)*

Cinéma en plein air

Open-air cinema festival, Parc de la Villette, free entry *(www.villette.com)*

August–September

Festival Classique au Vert

Open-air classical music festival Parc floral de Vincennes, free concerts Sat and Sun afternoons

September

Journées du Patrimoine (Heritage days)

Buildings and institutions that are normally closed to the public open their doors at various sites over the city *(3rd weekend of Sept)*

July: Tour de France

© Mark Kerr / Michelin

Mid-September–December

Festival d'automne

Fall arts festival, various venues (www.festival-automne.com)

October

Nuit Blanche (White Nights)

An all-night cultural festival *(see p 126, www.paris.fr)*

Fête des vendanges

Festival in Montmartre to celebrate bringing in the *quartier's* grape harvest *(2nd weekend of Oct)*

Prix de l'Arc de Triomphe

The prestigious horse race at the Hippodrome de Longchamp *(www.france-galop.com)* in the Bois de Boulogne

FIAC (International Contemporary Art Fair)

Grand Palais and Carrousel du Louvre *(www.fiacparis.com)* for amateur collectors and dealers

December

Salon du cheval de Paris

Major equestrian show for horse and rider, Villepinte *(www.salon-cheval.com)*

Fête de la Musique

Venue en ——— de Paris-nord

© Directphoto / age fotostock

PRACTICAL INFORMATION

WHEN TO GO

Paris is a wonderful city to visit at any time of the year. With its typical temperate climate, Paris experiences cold winters and hot summers, while both spring and fall can have glorious sunny days interspersed with gray and sometimes wet days. **Winters** can be severe although there is rarely much snow, and in December the streets and shop windows are bright with Christmas illuminations. If **spring** proves chilly, the blossoming parks and tree-lined boulevards provide plenty to enjoy. In **summer**, Parisians converge on the seasonal beach of Paris Plage and the open-air cafés along the Seine. The weather in the **fall** is generally crisp and sunny, and the city has a renewed air of energy and bustle.

KNOW BEFORE YOU GO

There is so much to see and do in Paris that planning your trip before you go is a good idea.

Useful websites

www.ambafrance-us.org – Practical information provided by the French Embassy in the US.
www.ambafrance-ca.org – The Cultural Service of the French Embassy in Ottawa, Canada.
www.visiteurope.com – Useful information on traveling to and around 34 European countries.
www.rendezvousenfrance.com – The official website of the French government's Tourist Office.
www.secretsofparis.com – Sightseeing, dining, accommodations, entertainment, shopping

advice, and a useful calendar of events.

Other websites worth a look include:
en.parisinfo.com
www.paris.fr
www.parisbalades.com

Tourist information

The main office in central Paris is:
Office du Tourisme et des Congrès de Paris – 25 rue des Pyramides, 75001 Paris. 08 92 68 30 00. www.parisinfo.com. Other information desks can be found at Gare de Lyon, Gare du Nord, Gare de l'Est, Anvers, and Parc des Expositions.

International visitors

American Embassy:
01 43 12 22 22
http://france.usembassy.gov
Australian Embassy:
01 40 59 33 00
www.france.embassy.gov.au
British Embassy:
01 44 51 31 00
http://ukinfrance.fco.gov.uk
Canadian Embassy:
01 44 43 29 00
www.canadainternational.gc.ca/france
Irish Embassy:
01 44 17 67 00
www.embassyofireland.fr
New Zealand Embassy:
01 45 01 43 43
www.nzembassy.com/france

Entry requirements

Passports – EU nationals entering France need only a national identity card. Nationals of other

14

countries must be in possession of a valid national passport. Loss or theft of your passport should be reported to the appropriate embassy or consulate and to the local police.

Visas – An entry visa is required for Canadian and US citizens who intend to stay for more than 3 months and for Australian and New Zealand citizens.
Apply to the French Consulate at home in good time before you travel.

Customs regulations

The US Customs and Border Protection's publication *Know Before You Go* for US citizens can be downloaded from www.cbp. gov. Americans can bring home, tax-free, up to US$800 worth of goods; Canadians up to CND$300; Australians up to AUS$400; and New Zealanders up to NZ$700. For EU citizens there are no limits to purchasing goods for personal use, but there are recommended allowances for alcoholic beverages and tobacco.
There are normally no restrictions on the importation of goods into France as long as they are for personal use and not for sale. For more information see:
http://www.douane.gouv.fr.

GETTING THERE
By Air

Paris is served by two major international airports: Roissy-Charles de Gaulle and Orly. Domestic flights are handled by Orly. For details on how to get to and from the airports and central Paris see the Aeroports de Paris website: www.adp.fr.

Roissy-Charles de Gaulle – 01 48 62 22 80, 08 92 68 15 15; www.adp.fr. 14.3mi/23km to the north of Paris on the A1.

Orly – 01 49 75 15 15; www.adp.fr.
6.8mi/11km to the south of Paris along the A6.

By Train

Paris has six mainline stations: Gare du Nord (for northern France, Belgium, Denmark, Germany, Holland, Scandinavia, and the UK); Gare de l'Est (for eastern France, Austria, Germany, Luxembourg); Gare de Lyon (for eastern and southern France, the Alps, Greece, Italy, Switzerland); Gare d'Austerlitz (for southwest France, Portugal, Spain); Gare Montparnasse (for western France and TGV to southwest France); Gare St-Lazare (for regional lines to northwest France).
For schedules and routes call **Rail Europe** 1 888 382 7245 in the US; 1 800 361 RAIL in Canada, or visit www.raileurope.com. Information on schedules can be obtained from the nationally owned French railway company **SNCF**:
www.sncf.fr. SNCF operates a telephone information, reservation, and prepayment service in English 7am–10pm (French time); call 08 36 35 35 39 from France, 00 8 36 35 35 39 when calling from outside France.
Eurostar trains arrive at Gare du Nord. For bookings and information call 01 233 617 575 or visit www.eurostar.com.

By Bus

Most buses coming into Paris arrive at the main Gare Routière at ave

15

General de Gaulle, Bagnolet. Métro Gallieni links it to the city center. For information about traveling all over Europe by bus: www.eurolines. com, 08 92 89 90 91 (in France). **Helplines** for disabled visitors 01 21 423 8479, and for deaf or hard-of-hearing visitors 01 21 455 0086.

By Car

It is relatively expensive to hire a car in France; it is best to arrange car rental before leaving or take advantage of fly-drive schemes. European cars usually have manual transmission but automatic cars are available—reservation in advance is recommended.

Visitors carrying a valid EU, international, or US (state) license may drive in France. A permit is available (US$10) from the **National Automobile Club** *(1 800 622 2136; www. nationalautoclub.com)* or contact a local branch of the American Automobile Association. Insurance cover is compulsory. Drivers must carry driving permits, international insurance cards, and vehicle registration cards. Regulations on drinking and driving (limited to 0.5g/l), wearing seatbelts, driving without a license, and speeding are strictly enforced—usually by an on-the-spot fine and/or confiscation of the vehicle.

All major autoroutes into Paris connect to a six-lane outer ringroad, the *boulevard périphérique*, 22mi/35km outside the city. Traffic merges onto the *périphérique* before filtering into the city center via the exits *(portes)*. Check which exit you need before setting off. Once inside Paris, the west-to-east Georges Pompidou motorway runs along the Right

Bank, facilitating the flow of cars through the capital.

For further information for all road-users, see http://about-france. com/travel.htm. For information on driving on motorways, which are often subject to a toll *(péage)*, see www.autoroute.fr.

GETTING AROUND

Paris has an excellent and inexpensive public transport system. RATP (Independent Paris Transport Authority) manages the urban Métro, bus, tram, and RER (Regional Express Rail) networks. For information: 08 92 68 77 14, www.ratp.fr.

If you plan to travel a lot by public transport it may be worthwhile to buy a tourist pass.

Paris Visite is a 1, 2, 3, or 5-day pass, valid on all modes of transport. The price depends on how many zones you need (zones 1–2, Paris; 3, near suburbs; 5, the airports, Disneyland, Versailles). Children 4–11 pay half fare and the pass offers discounts for tourist attractions.

One-day **Mobilis passes**, as well as weekly and monthly passes, are also available; for more information visit www.parisinfo.com (Transport).

By Métro

The Paris Métro is a cheap and efficient way of getting around the city. The network is comprehensive and the service frequent, operating from around 5.30am–12.30am (until 1.45am Fri, Sat and holidays). A book of ten t+ tickets *(un carnet)* costs 13.70€, child 6.85€: use one for each Métro, rail, or bus ride within Paris (you can transfer from one mode to another) and keep it with you (inspectors may ask to see it). Your ticket is valid for 90min from the time it's stamped. Tickets bought from bus drivers don't allow transfers. Children under 4 ride for free on a lap; under-10s pay half fare (demi-tarif).

Ticket offices open at 6.30am, but tickets can also be purchased from machines in stations and in tabacs (shops that sell cigarettes) and other shops with the RATP sign outside. Insert your Métro ticket in the turnstile and recover it, keeping it with you until you finish your journey.

By Bus

Bus routes are displayed in bus shelters and inside buses. A Grand Plan de Paris showing all bus routes is available from Métro stations. Buses normally operate 6.30am–8.30pm (Mon–Sat); designated lines operate until around 12.30am and on Sun and public holidays. **Night buses** (Noctilien) operate 1am–5.30am. On the bus, punch a single ticket in the machine by the door, but do not punch a pass—simply show it to the driver.

Bus lanes
Watch out for contraflow bus lanes where buses are traveling in the opposite direction to other vehicles—when crossing the road they can easily take you by surprise.

By Rail

Regional Express Network (RER) has five lines: **line A** runs from St-Germain-en-Laye, Poissy, and Cergy to Boissy-St-Léger and Marne-la-Vallée; **line B** from Robinson and

Validate rail tickets
If you are traveling by rail on an SNCF ticket (normally overground trains from a mainline station), just before you travel be sure to date-stamp it using one of the orange machines near the platforms.

St-Rémy-lès-Chevreuse to Roissy-Charles-de-Gaulle and Mitry-Claye; **line C** links Versailles (left bank), St-Quentin-en-Yvelines, Argenteuil, and Pontoise to Dourdan, Massy-Palaiseau, and St-Martin d'Etampes; **line D** runs from Orry-la-Ville and Coye to Crobeille, Melun, and Malesherbes; **line E** from St-Lazare to Villiers-sur-Marne and Chelles-Gournay.

Regular services run approximately 5am–1.15am. Métro tickets may be used for RER trains within the Métro system—outside these, special fares and tickets apply (including to airports, Versailles, and Disneyland-Paris).

By Taxi

Taxis are abundant in Paris and may be hired from the many taxi ranks close to road junctions and other frequented points.

Taxis may also be hailed in the street when the green light on the taxi is lit. The rate varies according to the zone and time of day (higher rates 8pm–6.30am). A supplementary charge is made for taxi pick-up at train stations, air terminals, and for heavy baggage or unwieldy parcels, as well as for a fourth person.

By Boat

Many tourist sites are close to the River Seine so hopping on and off the river bus makes sense. **Batobus** operates nearly year-round and stops at eight points along the Seine. Boats run every 15–30min 10am–7pm; check timetables, ticket prices, and stopping points at www.batobus.com. *See also Sports and Activities.*

By Bike

Paris has an ever-expanding network of cycle lanes. A north–south axis links the cycle path at Canal de l'Ourcq and Place de la Bataille-de-Stalingrad to Porte de Vanves. Another, running from east to west, joins the Bois de Vincennes and the Bois de Boulogne, both of which have a network of cycle paths complete with signposts. There are also combination bike-bus lanes. Designated areas where cyclists can leave their bikes are dotted around the capital; on Sun certain roads are closed to traffic for the benefit of pedestrians and cyclists.

Vélib' is a popular self-hire bike service in Paris, available 24hr, seven days a week. Visit www.velib.paris.fr for a downloadable leaflet. For further information, you can consult the *Paris à Vélo* (Paris by Bike) map available from tourist offices and bike shops, or look in listings publications *(see Entertainment listings, p 20). See also Sports and Activities.*

By Car

Everything you have heard about driving in Paris is true. Avoid it! Parking is restricted and while parking garages are well indicated, they are expensive. The Métro and

bus are usually faster than driving at most times of the day. Parking on the street, when authorized, is subject to a fee; tickets should be obtained from the ticket machines (*horodateurs*—unless you see the "CB" symbol with Visa/Mastercard logo on the machine, you'll need to pay with a prepaid *carte de stationnement*, which you can purchase at *tabacs*) and displayed inside the windshield on the driver's side; failure to display may result in a fine, or towing and impoundment. Visitors who arrive in Aug will find that it is easier to drive around the city then, but the riverside motorways are closed to traffic. Beware **axes rouges** (red routes) along main thoroughfares where parking is prohibited in order to maintain free flow of traffic (between Gare de Lyon and Gare de l'Est, via Bastille, République, quai des Célestins, and quai de la Rapée). Never, even in congested traffic, use the lanes reserved for buses and taxis—severe fines are always enforced.

BASIC INFORMATION
Accessibility

Disabled travelers – The *Touristes Quand Même* leaflet has detailed information about facilities for the disabled throughout Paris (available from the main tourist office in Paris).

The city's tourist office site, www.parisinfo.com, has further information for disabled travelers (Tourisme & Handicap). Few Métro and RER stations are easily accessible for wheelchairs—see the *Handicaps et Déplacements en Région Ile-de-France* leaflet on transport facilities available at main Métro and RER stations. Paris

MUST KNOW

Emergency: **Police 17, SAMU (paramedics)** ☎15, Fire *(pompiers)* ☎18

International Information, US/Canada: ☎00 33 12 11

International operator: ☎00 33 12 + country code

Local directory assistance: ☎118 008

Special-rate numbers in France begin with 0 800 (calls from within France only)

buses are slowly being equipped with access for wheelchairs, and all buses already have seats reserved for disabled and elderly persons. It is a legal requirement for taxi drivers to help people with disabilities to get in and out of their vehicle, and to carry guide dogs as passengers. This does not mean that all taxis are able to carry wheelchairs, so check when booking. Information for slow walkers, mature travelers, and others with special needs: can be found at www.access-able.com.

Accommodations
For a list of suggested accommodation *see Must Stay*.

Communications
Payphones in France use **prepaid phone cards** *(télécartes)*. *Télécartes* (50 or 120 units) can be bought in post offices, branches of France Télécom, *tabacs*, and newsagents. Calls can be received at phone booths where the blue bell sign is shown; the phone will not ring, so keep your eye on the little message screen.

Cell phones in France have numbers that begin with 06 or 07. The major networks are SFR, Orange, Bouygues, and Virgin. Some have their own pay-as-you-go services. Phones need to be GSM 90 or GSM 1800 to work in France.

Area codes – French telephone numbers have ten digits. Paris and Paris region numbers begin with 01. To call France from abroad, dial the country code (33) + 9-digit number (omit the initial 0). When calling abroad from France dial 00, then dial the country code followed by the area code and number of your correspondent.

Most hotels have **Internet** access available either in the room or business center, although this can be expensive. Internet cafés charge much more reasonable prices. RATP provides some free Internet booths *(bouquets)* at mainline stations. WiFi is prevalent in cafés, and free in all public parks.

Discounts
Significant discounts are available for senior citizens, students, youth under age 25, teachers, and groups for public transportation, museums, and monuments, and for some leisure activities such as the cinema (at certain times of day). Bring student or senior cards with you, and bring along some extra passport-sized photos for discount travel cards.
The **Paris Museum Pass** *(www.parismuseumpass.com)* is available from the Paris tourist office, and from participating museums and monuments.

Electricity
The electric current is 220 volts, 50 Hz. Circular two-pin plugs are

the rule. Adapters and converters should be bought before you leave home—they are on sale in most airports. If you have a rechargeable device (video camera, laptop, battery charger), read the instructions carefully or contact the manufacturer or shop. Sometimes these items only require a plug adapter; in other cases you must use a voltage converter as well or risk ruining your appliance.

Health

It is advisable to have comprehensive insurance cover as the recipient of medical treatment in French hospitals or clinics must pay the bill. Nationals of non-EU countries should check with their insurance companies about policy limitations. All prescription drugs should be clearly labeled; it is recommended that you carry a copy of the prescription.

US citizens concerned about travel and health can contact the International Association for Medical Assistance to Travelers: 716 754 4883, www.iamat.org. First aid, medical advice, and pharmacists' night service rota are available from pharmacies/drugstores *(pharmacie)* identified by the flashing green cross sign. Dentists are listed in the *Pages Jaunes* (Yellow Pages) under *Médecins Qualifiés*.

SOS Médecins – 01 47 07 77 77 (for emergencies).

Pharmacie Les Champs Dhéry – 84 ave des Champs-Élysées (Galerie des Champs-Élysées). Ⓜ George-V. Open 24hr, seven days a week, 01 45 62 02 41.

American Hospital – 63 blvd Victor-Hugo, 93 Neuilly-sur-Seine (4.6mi/7.5km from central Paris). 01 46 41 25 25.

British Hospital – 3 rue Barbès, 92 Levallois-Perret (5mi/8km). 01 46 39 22 22.

Money and currency exchange

Since Feb 2002, the euro has been the only currency accepted as a means of payment in France. It is divided into 100 cents or centimes. There are no restrictions on the amount of currency visitors can take into France; however, the amount of cash you may take out of France is subject to a limit, so visitors carrying a lot of cash should complete a currency declaration form on arrival.

American Express, Visa *(Carte Bleue)*, MasterCard/Eurocard, and Diners Club are widely accepted in shops, hotels, and restaurants, and gas stations. Before you leave home, learn your bank's emergency policies. In case of a lost or stolen credit card 24hr numbers are listed at most ATM machines. The loss or theft must also be reported to the local police who will issue a certificate to show to the credit card company.

The cheapest and most convenient way to change money is by using

Entertainment listings
For information about forth-coming entertainment events, movies, theater, and music listings, buy a copy of *Pariscope* or *L'Officiel de Spectacles* at one of the ubiquitous news kiosks, or visit www.offi.fr. For online listings in English visit: http://parisvoice.com and http://www.gogoparis.com.

cash dispensers (ATMs), known in France as DABs and easily recognized by the logo showing a hand holding a card. Money will be drawn from your account at a better rate than offered by banks and bureaux de change. Most ATMs will give a cash advance using Visa or MasterCard but this is a more expensive option. Exchange Bureaux can be found all over Paris—their commission rates vary, but must be clearly indicated.

Business hours

Large stores are open Mon–Sat 9am–6.30pm/7.30pm. Smaller shops may close during the lunch hour. Food shops—grocers, wine merchants, and bakeries—are open from around 7am–7.30pm; some open on Sun. Hypermarkets usually stay open until 9pm/10pm and are open Sun morning until 1pm. **Banks** are usually open 9am–4.30pm/5pm and are closed on Sun, Mon and possibly Sat; some branches open for limited transactions on Sat. Banks close early on the day before a public holiday.

Post offices

The main post offices *(bureaux de poste)* in the center of Paris are at 52 rue de Louvre *(24hr)* and 71 ave des Champs-Élysées. Post offices are open Mon–Fri 8am–7pm, Sat 8am–noon. Smaller branches often close at lunchtime *(noon–2pm)* and in the afternoon at 4pm. Stamps are also available from newsagents and *tabacs*.

Public holidays

Museums and other monuments may be closed or vary their hours of admission on public holidays.

France's public holidays are: New Year's Day *(Jan 1)*, Easter Mon *(Mon after Easter)*, Labor Day *(May 1)*, 1945 Victory Day *(May 8)*, Ascension *(40 days after Easter)*, Whit Mon *(50 days after Easter)*, Bastille Day *(Jul 14)*, Assumption *(Aug 15)*, All Saints' Day *(Nov 1)*, Remembrance Day *(Nov 11)*, Christmas Day *(Dec 25)*. In addition to the usual school vacations there are long mid-term breaks *(10–14 days)* in Feb and early Nov.

Smoking

Smoking is banned in all public places such as offices, universities, and railway stations, and including restaurants, cafés, and clubs etc.

Taxes and tipping

A sales tax is added to almost all retail goods. VAT refunds are available to visitors from outside the EU only if purchases exceed 175€ per store. The system works in large stores and other shops advertising "Duty Free." Show your passport and the store will complete a form that is stamped (at the airport) by customs. The refund is paid into your credit card account. Global Refund Tax Free Shopping is a service that, for a fee, simplifies the process of recovering tax; see www.globalrefund.com for more information. Since a service charge is automatically included in the prices of meals and accommodations in France, it is not necessary to tip in restaurants and hotels. However, if the service in a restaurant is especially good, an extra tip (a *pourboire*, rather than the *service*) is well-appreciated gesture.

WELCOME TO PARIS

Mention to a friend that you are visiting Paris for the weekend and you will hear small gasps of envy. High on everyone's personal "must see" list, few cities can match the charm and beauty of the capital of France. There's no shortage of reasons to visit Paris and the city makes it very easy to get around. Although a sprawling metropolis with suburbs reaching out across the Paris Basin, it is one of the easiest cities to explore because most of the major sights are within a relatively small central area. Farsighted city administrators have blessed it with a highly efficient and moderately priced transport system.

There is no shortage of things to do during your stay, but what better way to start the day than with a leisurely breakfast at a pavement café, a freshly baked *croissant au beurre* (naughty, but very nice), a glass of freshly squeezed orange juice, and a *café crème*. Yes, it's a cliché, but that doesn't detract one bit from the enjoyment and watching the French *art de vivre* is an additional delight. If you are in Paris for just a few days, you will then want to head for the main sights, and they won't disappoint. Take the Eiffel Tower for instance. Criticized by many during its construction, this elegant iron structure on the bank of the Seine is now the most iconic of all Parisian monuments, its graceful outline especially beautiful when lit up at night. From here it's a

short hop across the river to the Arc de Triomphe, down the Champs-Élysées to the Place de la Concorde, the Louvre, and finally the incomparable Notre-Dame. The banks of the Seine are lined with so many stunning and legendary monuments they have been collectively designated a UNESCO World Heritage Site.

As well as historic sights, Paris is a paradise for art lovers with a matchless range of works that you will have seen reproduced countless times before in books and magazines. Now you have the chance to see for yourself—*The Mona Lisa*, *The Venus de Milo*, Vermeer's *The Lacemaker*, Rodin's *The Thinker*, and of course many works by the Impressionists, from Van Gogh's *Bedroom in Arles* to Monet's *Water Lilies* series. And the buildings in which they are housed are almost as beautiful as the works themselves.

If you are fortunate enough to stay for a few more days, or if this is not your first visit, try venturing a little farther afield to find some of the city's less well-known sights. The fascinating Père-Lachaise cemetery or the newly fashionable district of Buttes-aux-Cailles are still only a short Métro ride away. Or take a boat trip with a differ-

On the terrace of a café, Saint-Germain-des-Prés

© S. Sauvignier / MICHELIN

© S. Sauvignier / MICHELIN

Paris Plage

ence from the marina at the port de Plaisance, and glide beneath the place de la Bastille, scene of Revolutionary ferment over two hundred years ago, to emerge on the serene Canal Saint-Martin, passing through locks and under bridges as you head toward the north of the city.

After sightseeing comes refreshment, equally central to the Paris experience. The city is a heaven for foodies, packed as it is with wonderful eateries, from *crêperies* and *salons de thés*, to grand restaurants offering true gourmet extravaganzas that will shrink your wallet as your waistline expands, with a host of bistros and brasseries in between. And when you need to rest weary limbs, you can join the Parisians in that other form of sightseeing—people-watching. Armed with *un petit café* or a glass of wine, you can sit back and watch the Parisian world go by.

When it is time to buy gifts to take home, again Paris won't disappoint. True there are supermarkets, but the city has been invaded far less by chain stores than many European cities and there are numerous independent stores specializing in all kinds of goods—fashion and accessories, something for the home,

chocolates, gourmet food, curios, and bric-a-brac. Markets are also dotted all over the city, usually a cluster of stalls in a square or lining part of a street, selling delicious fruit, bread, olives, cheese, and other goodies that might tempt you into enjoying an impromptu picnic in one of the city's parks and gardens, or one of the Paris Plage beaches along the Seine.

And as the sun goes down at the end of the day and the lights come on, romantic Paris is at its best. Take an evening stroll along the *quais* beside the river, or explore the narrow streets of Saint-Germain-des-Prés. Pause to watch a street entertainer, then dive into a bar for a *vin chaud* (in winter) or a cocktail. Why not visit one of the city's legendary cabaret venues or take in a movie. Music fans can enjoy an evening of live blues or jazz, then dance the night away to potent Brazilian rhythms or techno and hip-hop.

It will soon be morning and time to wake up to a new day in Paris. Leaving the city is always a wrench but with luck and skill you should have a collection of wonderful photographs to remind you of what a truly beautiful capital it is.

THE LEFT BANK

Synonymous with artistic, creative Paris, the districts immediately south of the Seine, which form the wider area known as the Left Bank (Rive Gauche), are full of shops, eateries, and delightful, secluded corners.

SAINT-GERMAIN-DES-PRÉS★★

A charming district, full of boutiques, small galleries, and antique stores. When not shopping you can visit beautiful churches, admire elegant mansions, or enjoy Impressionist art at the Musée d'Orsay.

FAUBOURG SAINT-GERMAIN★★

Ⓜ *Rue du Bac (line 12). RER: Musée d'Orsay (line C). Buses: 73, 83, 84, 94.*

Église St-Thomas d'Aquin – *Place St-Thomas-d'Aquin. Open Mon–Sat 8.30am–7pm, Sun 9am–noon, 4–7pm.* A beautiful 17C church tucked away behind rue du Bac, built on the site of a Dominican chapel. Inside are 17C and 18C paintings and an organ dating from 1771.

Palais Bourbon★ – *33 Quai d'Orsay. www.assemblee-nationale.fr.* The home of the French Legislative Assembly. The palace was built for the Duchess of Bourbon, daughter of Louis XIV, in the 1720s. The Prince de Condé, a later owner, enlarged and embellished it from 1764, and in 1827 it was converted for the Assembly. Inside, members sit in a semicircular chamber.

Rue de Grenelle – Named after the village of Grenelle, absorbed into the city long ago, rue de Grenelle is lined with grand houses, particularly **no. 118** with its garlanded windows, built in 1712, and **nos. 79, 85**, and **110**.

Rue de Varenne – The attractive old houses in this street include **nos. 47** (Italian Embassy) **72, 73, 78–80** (Ministry of Agriculture). Look for the shell carving over the door of **no. 56**. Built in 1721, **Hôtel Matignon** (no. 57) has been the French prime minister's official residence since 1958, while **Hôtel Biron★★** (no. 77) was loaned to sculptor **Rodin** in the 1900s and now houses the **Musée Rodin★★** *(see Great Galleries).*

Musée d'Orsay★★★
see Great Galleries

Pont des Arts leading to Institut de France

© S. Sauvignier / Michelin

Tour 1 – Around the Institut de France★★

Ⓜ *Pont-Neuf (line 7) Odéon (lines 4 and 10). Buses: 24, 27, 58, 70.*
✕ **Lunch stop** – Rue de Seine.

Quai des Grands-Augustins – Named after an Augustine monastery, it is the oldest quay in Paris (1313). Notice the fine mansions.

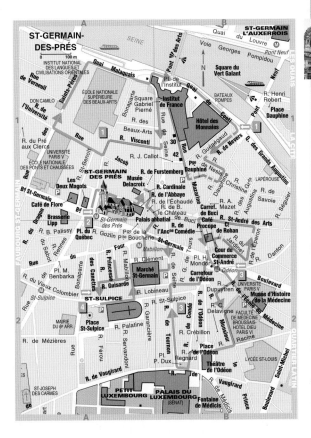

Rue Mazarine – A narrow street with small art galleries. Opera was presented for the first time in Paris at **no. 42** and Molière made his acting debut at **no. 12**.

Pont des Arts – Stroll over the city's first pedestrian bridge (rebuilt in the 1980s) and watch artists at work painting views of the river.

Institut de France★★ – *23 quai de Conti. 01 44 41 44 41. www.institut-de-france.fr. By appointment only.* The home of the Académie Française, guardian of the French language, and publisher of the official French dictionary. There are just 40 academicians at any one time; former members include Victor Hugo. Distinguished by its dome, the building is late 17C.

Hôtel des Monnaies et Médailles★ – *11 quai de Conti. 01 40 46 56 56. www.monnaiede paris.fr. Museum closed for renovations until 2014.*

Tour 2 – Saint-Germain-des-Prés

Ⓜ *St-Germain-des-Prés (line 4).* Buses: *39, 63, 70, 86, 87, 95, 96.* *See map p 25.*
✕ **Lunch stop** – Rue de Furstemberg and boulevard St-Germain.

Place du Québec – If you're not sure what to make of the pavement sculpture, it may help to know it represents ice breaking up.

Église St-Germain-des-Prés★★ – *3 place St-Germain-des-Prés. 01 55 42 81 33.* First built as a monastery chapel, this is the oldest church in Paris. It has been restored and enlarged considerably since. The heart of **Descartes** is interred here.

Rue de l'Abbaye – Look for Picasso's sculpture in a corner of place St-Germain-des-Près before admiring the impressive former abbot's palace (**palais abbatial**).

Musée Delacroix – *01 44 41 86 50. www.musee-delacroix.fr.* Open Mon, Wed–Sun 9.30am–5pm. This museum dedicated to the painter Eugène Delacroix is in the delightful square in the **rue de Furstemberg★**. You can visit his studio and apartment.

Rue Cardinale – Built in 1700 through the monastery's tennis court, **nos. 3–9** date from this time.

Boulevard St-Germain – The home of famous literary **Café des Deux Magots** and the **Café de Flore**, where intellectuals and artists of the 1950s and 1960s gathered. Brasserie Lipp (**no. 151**) is a popular celebrity venue.

Abbey of St-Germain-des-Prés

Founded in the 8C, the Benedictine abbey was used as a state prison from 1674. It was destroyed during the Revolution and the church turned into a saltpeter works. All that remains today are the church and the abbot's palace.

The old St-Germain Fair – Now the site of the **Marché St-Germain**, this was the St-Germain fairground. It was founded in 1482 by Louis XI, and as an early venue for an international trade fair it brought prosperity to Paris.

Tour 3 – Odéon★

Ⓜ *Odéon (lines 4 and 10). Buses: 58, 70, 86, 96. See map p 25.*
✕ **Lunch stop** – Carrefour de Buci.

Carrefour de l'Odéon (place Henri-Mondor) – **A popular meeting point,** the statue of **Danton**, the Revolutionary leader, stands on the site of his house.

Cour du Commerce-St-André★ – *Entrance via 130 blvd St-Germain, opposite Danton's statue.* **Dr Guillotin** demonstrated his decapitating machine using sheep here, and **Jean-Paul Marat** printed his Revolutionary paper. Today you can browse the pretty boutiques.

Cour de Rohan – A series of three courtyards from the mansion of the archbishops of Rouen. The noblewoman Diane de Poitiers lived in the fine Renaissance house overlooking the central courtyard.

Carrefour de Buci – The focal point of the Left Bank in the 18C (when it boasted a sedan chair rank, gibbet,

MUST SEE

and iron collar for criminals), today there are many fashion and antique stores and restaurants.

Rue de l'Ancienne-Comédie – The Comédie-Française, now at the Odéon theater, was based here.

Rue de l'École-de-Médecine – Now part of the university, the Brotherhood of Surgeons performed operations at **no. 5** until the 17C. Marat was murdered in his bath at **no. 30** rue de Cordeliers (the street's original name).

Musée d'Histoire de la Médecine – *Université René-Descartes, 12 rue École-de-Médecine. 01 40 46 16 93. Open Sept 1–Jul 15, 2–5.30pm. Closed Thu, Sun. www.univ-paris5.fr. 3.50€.* A fascinating collection of ancient and modern surgical instruments.

Rue Monsieur-Le-Prince – *01 43 26 08 56. www.augustecomte.org. Wed 2–5pm. Closed public holidays and Aug. 4€.* The museum in the apartment of the philosopher **Auguste Comte** is at **no. 10**.

Place de l'Odéon – The café at **no. 1** was a popular meeting place for writers in the 19C and early 20C.

Théâtre de l'Odéon – *Place de l'Odéon. 01 44 85 40 40. www.theatre-odeon.fr.* One of the national theaters of France, it dates back to 1782 although the present building is from 1807. Inside is a ceiling painted by André Masson in 1963.

Jardin du Luxembourg★★ *see Parks and Gardens*

Tour 4 – Around Saint-Sulpice★

Ⓜ *St-Sulpice (line 4), Mabillon (line 10). Buses: 48, 63, 70, 84, 95, 96. See map p 25.*
✕ **Lunch stop** – Place St-Sulpice.

Place St-Sulpice – The central Fountain of the Four Bishops (1844) by Visconti features four figures, each looking toward a different point of the compass.

Église de St-Sulpice★★ – *Rue St-Sulpice. 01 46 33 21 78. www.pss75.fr/saint-sulpice-paris. Open daily 7.30am–7.30pm. No charge.* The late Baroque building has a stunning interior with striking **murals★** by Delacroix, a fine **Lady Chapel★**, and notable **organ loft★**.

©yam / Fotolia.com

Église Saint-Sulpice

Marché St-Germain – Buy food and clothes at this covered market.

Rue Guisarde and rue Princesse – Pedestrianized streets that are perfect for a relaxed stroll during the day and lively and animated in the evening.

Rue des Canettes (ducklings) – Named after the relief at **no. 18**, this is another lively street in the evening, with bars and cafés.

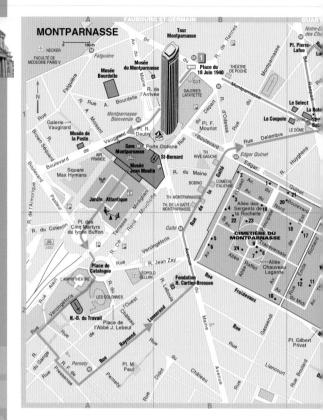

MONTPARNASSE

0 ——— 100 m

NECKER
FACULTÉ DE
MÉDECINE PARIS V

Falguière

Musée
Bourdelle

Musée
du Montparnasse

Tour
Montparnasse

Place du
18 Juin 1940

THÉÂTRE
DE POCHE

C.A.T.

GALERIES
LAFAYETTE

Départ

Le Select

La Coupole

LE DÔME

Galerie
Vaugirard

Musée de
la Poste

Montparnasse
Bienvenüe

Pl. R.
Dautry

Gare
Montparnasse

Porte Océane

St-Bernard

Boulevard

Musée
Jean Moulin

R. du Maine

BOBINO

COMÉDIE
ITALIENNE

TH. MONTPARNASSE

AIR
FRANCE

Square
Max Hymans

Jardin Atlantique

TH. DE LA GAÎTÉ
MONTPARNASSE

CIMETIÈRE DU
MONTPARNASSE

Pl. des
Cinq Martyrs
du lycée Buffon

Vercingétorix

Transversale

Allée
Chauveau
Lagarde

Froideveaux

Place de
Catalogne

LÉOPOLD
BELLAN

Fondation
H. Cartier-Bresson

L'AMPHITHÉÂTRE

LES COLONNES

N.-D. du Travail

Place de
l'Abbé J. Lebeuf

Pl. M.
Paul

Pl. Gilbert
Privat

Liancourt

MONTPARNASSE★★

Ⓜ *Montparnasse-Bienvenüe (lines
4, 6, 12, and 13). Buses: 28, 48, 58,
82, 89, 91, 92, 94, 95, 96.*
Renowned for the writers, thinkers,
and artists (such as Hemingway,
Picasso, and Sartre—many are
buried in the cemetery here) who
gravitated toward the *quartier* from
the early 1900s, Montparnasse is
still lively today, its famous cafés
and studios contrasting with
modern buildings such as the
Tour Montparnasse★★ and the
vast, busy rail station.

Tour 1 – Around
Montparnasse

✗ **Lunch stop** – Carrefour Vavin.

Place du 18-Juin-1940 – The
German governor surrendered
here on August 25, 1944. Now the
Centre Commercial shopping mall
pulls the crowd.

Tour Montparnasse★★ –
*01 45 38 52 56. www.tourmontpar
nasse56.com. Oct–Mar Sun–Thu
9.30am–10.30pm (Fri, Sat 11pm);
Apr–Sept 9.30am–11.30pm.
14.50€. Enjoy a magnificent*

Raymond-Losserand, named after the resistance fighter.

Fondation Henri Cartier-Bresson – *2 impasse Lebouis. 01 56 80 27 00. www.henricartier bresson.org. Open for exhibitions only. Check website for times.* A museum devoted to the work of this influential French photographer. One of the leaders of modern photojournalism, his evocative images speak volumes.

Rue de la Gaîté – A lively street of cabarets, dance halls, and theaters.

Cimetière du Montparnasse – *16 rue de Repos. 01 44 10 86 50. Open Mon–Sat 8am–5.45pm (Nov–Mar 5.15pm). No charge.* Opened in 1824, this tranquil spot is the last resting place for many of the famous, such as Serge Gainsbourg.

Carrefour Vavin (Place Pablo Picasso) – The famous haunts of the early 20C Bohemian set are all here—Le Dôme, La Rotonde, Le Sélect, and La Coupole

Rue de la Grande-Chaumière – At **no. 10** Gauguin, Manet, and Whistler worked in the Académie Charpentier. The famous art store Sennelier is along here too.

Rue Notre-Dame-des-Champs – At **no. 53** is the **Lucernaire**, an experimental theater with two cinemas. Note the sculptures on the façade of **no. 82**. Fernand Léger lived in the atelier at **no. 86**.

Place Pierre-Lafue – Pass the statue *Hommage au Capitaine Dreyfus* and onto boulevard Raspail to Rodin's sculpture **Balzac**.

panorama★★★ of Paris and its suburbs from the 56th floor and rooftop restaurant.

Gare Montparnasse – A busy train terminal and Métro interchange, but on the roof in the gardens of the **Jardin Atlantique★** all is calm. *See For Kids.*

Place de Catalogne – An ampitheater and a vast fountain lie behind the striking Neoclassical buildings. Take a peek at the unusual **Église Notre-Dame-du-Travail** before following **rue**

Tour 2 – Denfert-Rochereau

Ⓜ *Denfert-Rochereau (lines 4 and 6). RER: line B. Buses: 38, 68. See map pp 28–29.*
✕ **Lunch stop** – Place Denfert-Rochereau.

Place Denfert-Rochereau – The buildings decorated with sculpted friezes are remnants of late 18C city gates and toll houses. The square is named after a 19C colonel.

🔲 **Les Catacombes★** – *1 place Denfert-Rochereau. 01 43 22 47 63. www.catacombes.paris.fr. Open Tue–Sun 10am–5pm. Closed public holidays. 8€.* Housed in the remains of ancient quarries, millions of human remains were transferred here from overcrowded cemeteries. Wander through tunnels stacked high with bones, arranged in neat rows and patterns.

Rue Froidevaux – At **nos. 21–23** are 1920s artists' studios.

Rue Campagne-Première – Many artists lived here, including Modigliani (**no. 3**), Man Ray (**no. 31bis**), and at **no. 17** Picasso. **No. 11** was immortalized in Godard's 1960 film *Breathless*.

SÈVRES-BABYLONE★

Ⓜ *Sèvres-Babylone (lines 10 and 12). Buses: 39, 68, 70, 83, 87, 94.*

Boulevard Raspail – The ornate **Hôtel Lutétia** *(no. 45)* stands at the corner with rue de Sèvres. Rough blocks of rock at **nos. 52–54** mark the site of the former prison where Captain Dreyfus was held in 1894.

Carrefour de la Croix-Rouge – *Intersection of rue de Sèvres and rue du Cherche-Midi.* Once the site of a pagan temple, the Christian cross was installed here in the 16C.

Chapelle Notre-Dame-de-la-Médaille-Miraculeuse – *140 rue du Bac.* The Virgin was said to have appeared to a novice nun here in 1830, requesting that a medal be struck bearing the Virgin's image. The nun was later beatified.

Rue du Cherche-Midi – A long street of grand houses. Make a brief detour into rue Jean Ferrandi to see former artists' studios.

Rue des Saints-Pères – The former 17C chapel to St-Pierre (**no. 51**) is now home to the Ukrainian Catholic church of St Vladimir the Great.

Les Catacombes

© Roetting / Pollex / Look / Photononstop

PORT-ROYAL
RER: Port-Royal (line B).
Buses: 38, 83, 91.

Musée de l'Eglise du Val-de-Grace – *277 bis rue St-Jacques. 01 39 30 72 72. Open Tue–Wed, Sat–Sun noon–5pm. 4.60€.* Originally a Jansenist convent, it has also been a prison and a children's home. It is now part of a public assistance hospital.

Église du Val-de-Grâce★★ – *1 place Alphonse-Laveran. Open Mon–Sat 2–6pm, Sunday 9am–noon, 2–6pm.* This beautiful baroque church is now part of the Val-de-Grâce military hospital complex. It was the gift of Anne of Austria on the birth of her son Louis XIV. Inside the **dome★★** is painted with an impressive fresco by Mignard and there is an elaborate baldaquin by Gabriel Le Duc over a nativity scene.

Fontaine de l'Observatoire★ – Look out for this grand fountain in the gardens to the right of the RER station.

Observatoire de Paris★ – *61 ave de l'Observatoire. 01 40 51 22 21. www.obspm.fr.* The Paris meridian runs through this building which, completed in 1671, is the oldest functioning observatory in

the world. The building's walls face the four points of the compass. Among the discoveries made here was the dimensions of the solar system in 1672.

LES GOBELINS
Ⓜ *Les Gobelins (line 7).*
Buses: 27, 47, 83, 91.

La Butte-aux-Cailles – In 1783 Pilâtre de Rozier landed in this area, then on the outskirts of Paris, after the first free-flight in a hot air balloon. Today it has an intimate village-like feel with trendy bars and cafés.

Manufacture des Gobelins

©Paris Tourist Office – Photographer: Raymond Mesnildrey

Manufacture des Gobelins★ – *42 ave des Gobelins. 01 44 54 19 33. www.mobiliernational.culture. gouv.fr. Open Tue–Sun 11am–6pm. 6€.* The *manufacture* (factory) was the royal tapestry and furniture works, and still produces a limited number of tapestries today. The method has changed little since the 17C—consequently new orders take a while to complete!

Square René-le-Gall – *Rue Corvisart.* The square is now occupied by pretty gardens. Look out for the owl plaque, with ammonites for eyes. Below ground, the River Bièvre winds through tunnels. Once polluted by waste from the local industries it was covered over in 1910.

The tapestry workshops

The earliest of the great tapestry workshops were founded on the bank of the River Bièvre in 1440 by Jean Gobelin. They made the tapestries for Louis XIV's splendid palaces here.

THE LEFT BANK

THE LATIN QUARTER★★

🚇 St-Michel (line 4), Cluny-La Sorbonne (line 10). RER: St-Michel -Notre-Dame (lines B and C), Luxembourg (line B). Buses: 21, 27, 38, 82, 83, 84, 85, 86, 87, 89. Well known for its winding streets thronged by students, and bookstores and budget eateries, the Quartier Latin has been the home of France's major universities, including the Sorbonne, since the late 12C. It was also the focal point of the student revolt and street battles of 1968. The Panthéon and the church of St-Étienne-du-Mont are also major landmarks.

Tour 1 – Around the Sorbonne

✕ **Lunch stop** – Boulevard St-Michel.

Quai St-Michel – Enjoy the view of Notre-Dame as you browse the *bouquiniste* stalls selling secondhand books, posters, and all sorts of curios. Make sure you glance down the **rue du Chat qui Pêche** (the fishing cat!)—it's a perfect example of the medieval character of the area.

Place St-Michel – Built during the reign of Napoléon III, the square is a popular meeting place. The bronze statue of St Michel over the fountain is by Gabriel Davioud.

Around St-Séverin – This area is perhaps one of the oldest quarters of Paris: **rue de la Harpe** was the main north–south Gallo-Roman road. Today the small, narrow streets around here are crowded with restaurants, many of which offer Greek meals.

Église St-Séverin★★ – *Rue des Prêtres St-Séverin. 01 42 34 93 50.* Although dating from the 13C, the 15C Gothic architecture is a highlight: the double **ambulatory★★** encircling the chancel and the **stained glass★** in the upper windows. Outside are the restored ruins of the **cloister**.

🛥 **Boulevard St-Michel** – Ideal for a browse or rest-stop with its café terraces and bookstores.

Musée National du Moyen Âge★★ see Major Museums
Jardin medieval see For Kids

Rue des Écoles – The entrances of the Collège de France and the Sorbonne are along here.

La Sorbonne – Founded in 1257 by King Louis IX for 16 poor students to study theology, the Sorbonne was named after Robert de Sorbon, his confessor, and became a major French university. Its facilities include 22 lecture halls, 37 tutorial rooms, 240 laboratories, and an astronomy tower.

Église de la Sorbonne★ – 17 rue de la Sorbonne. www.paris-sorbonne.fr. Open only for group tours. Designed between 1635 and 1642, it is the oldest building of the Sorbonne.

Rue Soufflot – At the far end of this road is the **Panthéon★★**, but don't miss **no. 3**, with its mythological statues and the old apothecary-style pharmacy.

Panthéon★★ see Landmarks

Tour de Calvin – 19–21 rue Valette. This tower is the remains

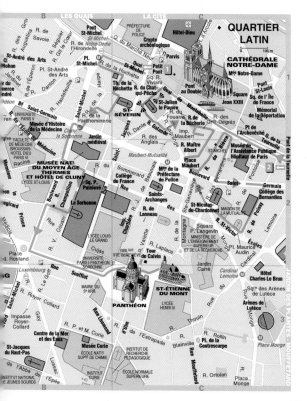

of Fortet Collége, where the Catholic League was founded in 1585, and which went on to expel Henri III from Paris in 1588.

Église St-Étienne-du-Mont★★ –
Place Ste-Geneviève. www.saint etiennedumont.fr. Open Tue–Sat 10am–noon, 4–7.45pm, Sun 10am–12.45pm, 4.30–7.45pm.
This unique church is home to the only **rood screen★★** in Paris. Built between 1492 and 1626 in the Gothic style, it venerates Saint Geneviève. Other features are the **façade★★**, the vaulting above the transept, the **stained glass★**, and **the pulpit★**, supported by a figure of Samson. In the cloisters are 17C **stained-glass windows★**.

JUSSIEU★

Ⓜ *Jussieu (lines 7 and 10), Cardinal Lemoine (line 10), Place Monge (line 7). Buses: 24, 63, 67, 86, 87, 89.*

La Mosquée★ (The Mosque) –
Place du Puits-de-l'Ermite. 01 45 35 97 33. Guided tours. www. mosqueedeparis.net. Open Sun–Thu 9am–noon, 2–6pm. Closed Muslim feast days. 3.50€. Explore the exotic walled compound

of the 1920s Hispano-Moorish buildings.

Arènes de Lutèce – *Rue des Arènes. Open 9am–9pm (summer); 8am–5pm (winter). No charge.*
The ruins of a Gallo-Roman amphitheater in the heart of Paris; they lay buried for 500 years until the rue Monge was laid in 1869.

Pierre and Marie Curie University – *Place Jussieu.* Once a wine market, the square is now lined with university buildings.

Collections des Minéraux★ –
Pierre and Marie Curie University, 4 place Jussieu. 01 44 27 52 88. www.amis-mineraux.fr. Open Wed–Mon 1–6pm. Closed Jan 1, Easter, May 1, Jul 14, All Saints Day, Dec 25. 5€. Discover dazzling crystals, rare stones, and beautiful rocks.

Hôtel Charles Le Brun – *49 rue Cardinal-Lemoine.* A fine building, once home to the painter Antoine Watteau (1718) and the naturalist Georges Louis Leclerc Buffon (1766). Buffon completed his treatise on natural history here.

Musée de la Sculpture en plein air – *Quai Saint-Bernard. Square Tino-Rossi. Year-round, 24hr.* A riverside garden featuring sculpture by Brancusi, Stahly,

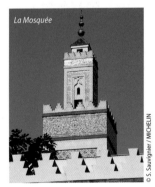

La Mosquée

© S. Sauvignier / MICHELIN

MUST SEE

Zadkine, and Rougemont, among others.

MOUFFETARD★
🅼 *Censier-Daubenton (line 7). Buses: 47, 89.*

Église St-Médard – *141 rue Mouffetard. Open Tue–Sun. Closed May 1 and 8, Pentecost, and Nov 11.* The church can be entered from **rue Daubenton**. Completed in 1655, it contains a number of fine paintings from the French school. Look out for the fine 16C triptych behind the pulpit.

Rue Mouffetard★ – A lively street with a regular market, look above the frontages of the shops and cafés to see the old houses and painted signs, such as **nos. 69** and **122**. At **nos. 104** and **101** are the entrances to passage des Postes and passage des Patriarches.

10 rue Vauquelin – **Pierre and Marie Curie** isolated radium here in October 1898.

Institut du Monde arabe★ *see New Paris*

Jardin des Plantes★★ *see Parks and Gardens*

Tour 2 – Maubert
🅼 *Maubert-Mutualité (line 10). Buses: 47, 63, 87. See map pp 32–33.* ✕ **Lunch stop** – Rue du Fouarre.

Quai de la Tournelle – There's a great **view★★★** of Notre-Dame from the bridge. The ultra-expensive Tour d'Argent restaurant at **no. 15** dates back to 1582.

Quai de Montebello – Wood for building and heating was brought by raft to the Port-aux-Bûches, between the Petit Pont and **Pont au Double** in the Middle Ages.

Square René-Viviani – Discover one of the oldest trees (1601) in Paris in this square named after a French politician. There is a good **view★★★** of the church of St-Julien-le-Pauvre and Notre-Dame.

Église St-Julien-le-Pauvre★ – *1 rue St-Julien-le-Pauvre. 01 43 54 52 16. Open Mon–Sat 9.30am–1pm, 3–6.30pm.* Built around the same time as Notre-Dame, this beautiful old church was named after a medieval bishop, also known as St Julien the Poor because he gave away so much money.

Rue Galande – Now known more for its bars, this road has a number of medieval architectural features—a carved stone over the door of **no. 42** shows St Julian the Hospitaller in his boat.

Winding streets – At **31 rue du Fouarre** medieval students listened to lectures seated on straw *(fouarre)*. In **Impasse Maubert** Marquise de Brinvilliers concocted poisons in the 17C, below **rue Maître-Albert** underground passages once hid outlaws, **Place Maubert** has long been a rallying point for students, and **rue de Bièvre** lies over the stream of the same name used by tanners and boatmen. **Rue de Poissy** was laid through the gardens of a college and **St-Nicolas-du-Chardonnet** thistles *(chardons)* was built in a field of thistles.

PARIS CENTER

Forming a focal point as it winds its way across the center of the city, the River Seine divides Paris into the Left and Right Banks. The city's principal districts radiate out to the north and south of the river.

THE ISLANDS★★★

Several iconic monuments jostle for position on the islands in the middle of the Seine. At the heart of Paris geographically and historically, the **Île de la Cité★★★** is where the Parisii settled in around 200 BC. The **Île St-Louis★★** is a residential area with quirky gift and gourmet food shops.

Tour 1 – Île de la Cité
Ⓜ *Pont Neuf (line 7).*
✕ **Lunch stop** – Place Dauphine.

Pont Neuf★ – In spite of its name (New Bridge), this is the oldest of the Parisian bridges and one of the most beautiful. Built between 1578 and 1604, it carried the first road in Paris to benefit from paved areas separating traffic from pedestrians.

Square du Vert-Galant – Down the steps behind the statue of Henri IV, this delightful stretch of greenery is named after the king—it was Henri's roving eye that earned him the nickname *le vert galant* ("the Green Gallant").

Place Dauphine★ – Built by **Henri IV**, this tranquil square dates back to 1607. It was named after the Dauphin (the title given to the heir to the French throne), the future Louis XIII.

Today, just a few of the façades retain their original features, such as **no. 14**.

Quai des Orfèvres – During the 17C and 18C, this was the jewelers' quarter. More recently, **No 36** was the headquarters of the Paris branch of the Police Judiciaire.

Palais de Justice★
Entrance Cour du Mai. 01 44 32 52 52. Open Mon–Sat 8.30am–6pm. Closed public holidays.

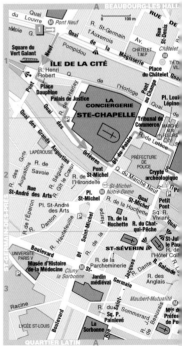

Dating back to the time of the Romans, the building was used as a royal palace until the mid 14C. It is now the center of the French judicial system housing the law courts and **Sainte-Chapelle★★★**.

Cour du Mai – This courtyard takes its name from the ancient custom whereby clerks of the court planted a tree from one of the royal forests each year on May 1.

Galerie Marchande – These galleries once echoed to the comings and goings of lawyers, the accused, and souvenir salesmen.

Salle des Pas-Perdus – In this lobby a tortoise at the foot of the monument to 19C barrister Berryer makes silent comment on the habitual delays of the legal system. The former apartment of Louis IX at the end of the lobby was used by the Revolutionary Tribunal to sentence thousands to death. It now houses the First Civil Court.

Île de la Cité and the Seine

© Jérôme Delaye / Fotolia.com

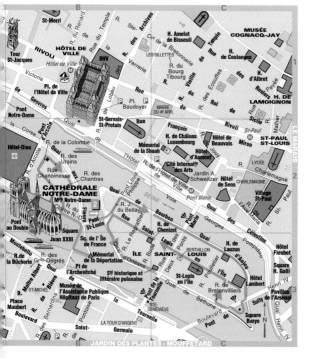

Conciergerie★★

Entrance blvd du Palais. 01 53 73 78 50. Open Mar–Oct 9.30–6pm; Nov–Feb 9am–5pm. Closed Jan 1, May 1, Nov 1 and 11, Dec 25. Entry 8.50€. Combined ticket with Sainte-Chapelle, 12.50€.

Part of the Palais de Justice complex, the Conciergerie served as a prison from the 14C to 1914. Ordinary citizens and aristocrats alike were imprisoned here during the Revolution, usually awaiting "Madame La Guillotine." The prison's history is given on the first floor.

Salle des Gens d'Armes★★ – A superb vaulted Gothic chamber that formed the great hall of the original royal palace.

Kitchen – Between 2,000 and 3,000 people a day were fed from here when the building was part of the royal palace.

Galerie des Prisonniers – Where penniless prisoners would sleep on the bare ground, unlike the rich who could pay for their own cell.

Chapelle des Girondins – This chapel was transformed into a communal cell where prisoners heard mass through the grille in the upper story.

Cour des Femmes – A small courtyard is where women prisoners were allowed out during the day. A door on the right leads to a reconstruction of Marie-Antoinette's simple cell.

Victims of the guillotine

The Conciergerie played host most famously to Marie-Antoinette, but also to Charlotte Corday and Madame du Barry. Other notable victims of the Revolution included Georges Danton and Robespierre.

Sainte-Chapelle★★★
see Landmarks

Place Louis-Lépine – A colorful **flower market** is held here *(Mon–Sat)*, with a **bird market** on Sunday. The Préfecture de Police is on one side of the square and the **Hôtel Dieu**, the oldest hospital in Paris, on another.

Notre-Dame★★★ *see Landmarks*

Ancien quartier du Chapitre – Take a trip back in time to the 11C and 12C and explore the streets north of Notre-Dame. **Nos. 22** and **24 rue Chanoinesse** are the last two medieval canons' houses, while in **rue de la Colombe**, you can see traces of a Gallo-Roman wall. At the end of the **rue des Ursins** are the remains of a medieval chapel where priests celebrated mass secretly during the Revolution.

Square Jean-XXIII – The area to the rear of Notre-Dame was crowded with buildings until they were razed to the ground during a riot in 1831. It was transformed into a formal garden with a neo-Gothic fountain, opened in 1844.

Square de l'Île-de-France – The former site of the Paris municipal morgue. Until 1910, it was a kind of macabre tourist attraction where bodies (including those drowned) were laid out to be identified.

Mémorial de la Déportation – *01 46 33 87 56. Open Apr–Sept 10am–noon, 1.15–7pm; Oct–Mar 10am–noon, 2–5pm.* This moving memorial is to those deported from France to the Nazi concentration camps during World War II.

Tour 2 – Île Saint-Louis★★

🅜 *Pont Marie (line 7).*
See map pp 36–37.
✕ **Lunch stop** – Rue St-Louis-en-l'Île.

Pont St-Louis – Built in 1970 to replace the original bridge linking the two islands and now closed to traffic, this is a good place to appreciate the **views★★** of Notre-Dame and the Hôtel de Ville.

Quai de Bourbon – Look out for two magnificent town houses (**nos. 15** and **19**). Sculptor Camille Claudel's studio was at **no. 19**.

Pont Marie★ – One of Paris's oldest bridges and it still looks more or less as it did at the end of the 18C.

Quai d'Anjou – Ford Madox Ford founded his literary journal *The Transatlantic Review* at **no. 29**. Painter, sculptor, and caricaturist Honoré Daumier lived at **no. 9**, and the Marquise de Lambert, hostess of a 18C literary salon at **no. 27**.

Hôtel de Lauzun – *No. 17. Limited guided tours.* Built in 1657 and named after the Duke of Lauzun, poet Théophile Gautier lived here.

Square Barye – This delightful small "square" is the last trace of the terraced garden once belonging to the financier, Bretonvilliers.

Pont de Sully – From the southern section of the bridge (1876), there's a good **view★** looking west to Notre-Dame. In the 17C there was a popular bathing beach here.

Hôtel Lambert★ – *No. 2.* Built in 1640 by Le Vau, this mansion was decorated by Le Sueur and Le Brun. In 1975 it became Baron Guy de Rothschild's Paris residence.

Église St-Louis-en-l'Île★ – *No. 19 bis. 01 46 34 11 60. Open Tue–Sun 9am–noon, 3–7pm.* You can spot this church by the unusual clock fixed to the wall outside and its pierced spire. Also designed by Le Vau, the interior is richly decorated in the baroque style.

Hôtel de Chenizot – *No 51.* It was the archbishop's residence in the 19C. Look for the head of a faun carved over the fine doorway in the beautifully ornamented façade.

Quai d'Orléans – Another fine **view★★** toward Notre-Dame and south toward the Left Bank.

Société historique et littéraire polonaise★

6 quai d'Orleans. 01 55 42 83 85. Open Thu 2.15–5.15pm, Sat 9am–noon. Closed Aug, public holidays. Three museums are housed in this 17C building, all devoted to prominent Poles—the **Adam-Mickiewicz Museum** has documents and mementoes of the 19C poet. The **Salle Chopin** includes some of the composer's original manuscripts. The **Musée Boleslas Biegas** has works by this 21C surrealist artist along with other Polish artists.

LE MARAIS★★★

ⓜ **Chemin-Vert (line 8), St-Paul
(line 1). Buses: 20, 29, 69, 76, 96.**
Containing the oldest and most
beautiful square in Paris—place
des Vosges—the historic Marais is
full of narrow streets, small shops,
cafés, museums, and galleries—just
about everything the visitor could
want. It is also home to Paris's
Jewish quarter.

Tour 1 – Southern Marais
✕ **Lunch stop** – Rue des Barres.

Église St-Paul-St-Louis – *99 rue
Saint-Antoine. 01 42 72 30 32.
Open Mon–Fri 8am–8pm, Sat
8am–7.30pm, Sun 9am–8pm.*
Completed in 1627, this church
was built by the Jesuits and
modeled on the Gesu church in
Rome. Spacious and well lit inside,
much of its rich decoration was
lost in the Revolution. The twin
shell-shaped stoups were given
by Victor Hugo who lived in the
nearby place des Vosges.

Village St-Paul – As the maze of
courtyards here is known. They
contain many antique shops,
which are great for browsing.

Rue des Jardins St-Paul –
Look out for the surviving frag-
ment of the **Philippe Auguste
City Wall**, built around 1200.

Hôtel de Sens★ – *1 rue du Figuier.*
The vivacious **Queen Margot**,
Henri IV's first wife, lived here
from 1605 on her return from
exile. A glorious medieval
building, complete with small
turrets, today it houses the
Forney Library (*01 42 78 14
60; open Tue–Fri 1.30–8pm, Sat*

*10am–8pm; closed public holidays
and 2 weeks in Jul; temporary
exhibitions 4€*) devoted to the
decorative and fine arts, and
industrial techniques.

Hôtel d'Aumont – *7 rue de Jouy.*
A detour will take you to the
magnificent former residence of

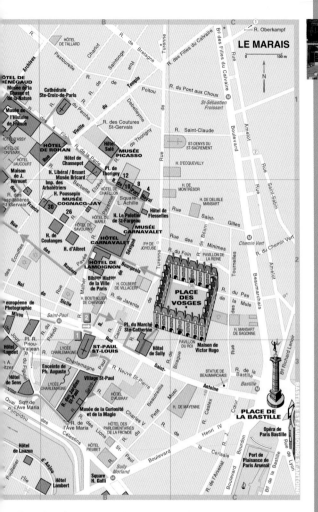

the Dukes of Aumont, now home to the Paris administrative court.

Mémorial de la Shoah – *17 rue Geoffroy-l'Asnier. 01 42 77 44 72. www.memorialdelashoah.org. Open Sun–Fri 10am–6pm (Thu 10pm). Closed on Jewish feast days.* This is dedicated to the millions of Jews lost in the Holocaust. The **Mur des Noms** is a wall bearing the names of the 76,000 Jews deported from France and an eternal flame is kept lit in the crypt. Exhibitions and archive material relate their history.

Église St-Gervais-St-Protais★ – *Place St-Gervais*. A basilica has stood on this site since the 6C, but most of the present building dates from the 16C and 17C. Inside is a fine organ, built in 1601 and, unusually, played by eight generations of one family between 1656 and 1826.

Rue François Miron – This was once a Roman road through an area of marsh. Two 15C half-timbered houses can be found at **nos. 13** and **11**. The **Hôtel de Beauvais★** at no. 68 was built in the 17C for Catherine Bellier, first woman of the bedchamber to Anne of Austria, and her husband Pierre Beauvais. In 1763, the seven-year-old Mozart stayed here with his father and sister.

Maison européenne de la Photographie – *5–7 rue de Fourcy. 01 44 78 75 00. www. mep-fr.org. Open Wed–Sun 11am–7.45pm. Closed public holidays. 8€.* Housed in a mansion built in 1704 for a royal tax collector, this is a cutting-edge photographic collection dating from 1958 onward.

Tour 2 – Around la place des Vosges
See map pp 40–41.

Place des Vosges

© Pi Ju Yang / Bigstockphoto.com

✕ **Lunch stop** – Place du Marché-Sainte-Catherine.

Place du Marché-Sainte-Catherine★ – This small, lively square has a village-like atmosphere and is named after the 13C priory dedicated to St Catherine.

Rue St-Antoine – It was in this street that in 1559 **Henri II** received a fatal blow to his eye during a tournament. The man who dealt the blow, his Scots captain of the guard Montgomery, took to his heels but was caught and executed. No. 62, **Hôtel de Sully★** was built in 1625 *(01 44 61 20 00; access to the courtyard and gardens only; open Tue–Sun 10am–6pm).* Appropriately enough, it now houses the Historic Buildings Commission. The magnificent Louis XIII inner **courtyard★★** is behind the restored main gate.

Place des Vosges★★★ – King Henri IV commissioned this symmetrical square surrounded by 36 beautiful mansions. Completed in 1612, it was the height of fashion and elegance, and a venue for courtly parades and festivities. Today it's a perfect place to stroll and browse the shops beneath the colonnades, or to take lunch at a restaurant. At no. 6 is the **Maison de Victor Hugo★** *(01 42 72 10 16; open Tue–Sun 10am–6pm; closed public holidays).*

Hôtel de Lamoignon★ – *24 rue Pavée.* Built c 1585 for Diane de France, the legitimized daughter of Henri II, it became the **Bibliothèque historique de la ville de Paris** in 1793—

documents relating to the Revolution are held here.

Rue des Rosiers – This colorful street is at the heart of the Jewish quarter, with kosher bakeries and restaurants, and various specialty food stores.

Église de Notre-Dame-des-Blancs-Manteaux – 12 rue des Blancs-Manteaux. 01 42 72 09 37. There are some beautiful examples of woodwork inside, including a fine Flemish **pulpit**★ in this church named after the white habits worn by the Augustinian monks who founded a convent here.

Musée d'Art et d'Histoire du Judaïsme★★ – *Hôtel de Saint-Aignan, 71 rue du Temple. 01 53 01 86 60. www.mahj.org. Open Mon–Fri 11am–6pm, Sun and public holidays 10am–6pm. Closed Jan 1, May 1, Dec 25, Jewish holidays. 8€.* Take a detour to this museum housed in an historic mansion, which gives an in-depth insight into Jewish culture, religion, and the diaspora, via documents, paintings, photos, and objects.

Rue des Archives – More fine mansions line this road, including the 14C **Hôtel de Soubise**★★ at no 60. The **Musée de l'Histoire de France**★ and part of the French national archives are housed here *(01 40 27 60 96; www.archives-nationales.culture.gouv.fr; open Mon, Wed–Fri 10am–5.30pm, Sat–Sun 2–5.30pm). 3–6€.* Highlights include documents signed by important historical figures such as Marie-Antoinette, and the **Chambre de la Princesse**

and the **appartements**★★, rooms occupied by 18C aristocrats, which appear little changed. The hunting museum **Musée de la Chasse** *(01 53 01 92 40; www.chassenature.org; open Tue–Sun 11am–6pm; Wed until 9.30pm; closed public holidays; 8€)* is in **Hôtel de Guénégaud**★★ at no. 60.

Cathédrale Ste-Croix-de-Paris★ – *Rue Charlot. 01 44 59 23 50. Open Sun 10am–1pm, weekdays by appointment with the parish priest.* Now used by the Armenian community, this was originally part of a Capuchin monastery. Inside is a fine **statue**★ of St Francis of Assisi by Germain Pilon (16C).

Hôtel de Rohan★★ – *87 rue Vieille-du-Temple. 01 40 27 60 96. Open Wed–Mon 10am–5.30pm, Sat–Sun 2.30–5.30pm. Closed public holidays. 3€.* The former residence of four cardinals of the Rohan family. The superb interior, including the cardinals' **appartements**★, dates from the1750s. Part of the national archives are housed here.

Picasso Museum★★ in **Hôtel Salé** *see Major Museums.*

Rue du Parc-Royal – Beautiful 17C mansions line the street opposite Square Léopold-Achille, such as **nos. 4, 8, 10**, and **12**.

Musée Carnavalet★★ in **Hôtel Carnavalet**★★ *see Major Museums.*

If you would like to go shopping after you have finished the tour, try the fashion-lover's paradise around **rue Vieille-du-Temple** and **rue du Roi-de-Sicilie**.

PARIS CENTER

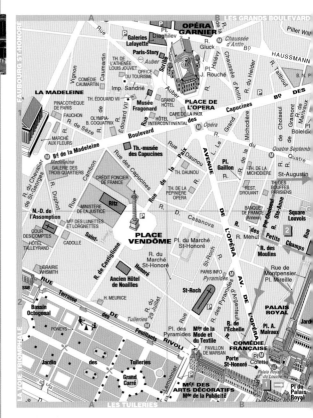

PALAIS-ROYAL★★

The magnificent Palais-Royal
enjoys a suitably grandiose setting
not far from the Louvre and the
river in this historic part of Paris.
As well as kings, queens, and
cardinals, the area has links with
the theater—the Théâtre Français
(now the Comédie-Française) and
the Théâtre du Palais-Royal were
opened here in the 1790s.

Tour 1 – Around the
Palais-Royal

Ⓜ *Palais-Royal–Musée du
Louvre (lines 1 and 7). Buses: 21, 27,*

69, 76, 81, 95.
✕ **Lunch stop** – Rue St-Honoré.

Place du Palais-Royal – The
square is flanked by the elegant
Palais-Royal and the great **Louvre**
museum (see *Major Museums*).
Augustin Pajou designed the 18C
carvings of military trophies and
allegorical figures that decorate
the palace.

Palais-Royal★ – *Place du Palais-
Royal. Palace closed. Access to
courtyard and arcades.* Completed
in 1629, it was originally built

for Cardinal Richlieu when he was prime minister of France, but became a royal palace on his death when he bequeathed it to Louis XIII. It now houses a number of government offices. In the Cour d'honneur the black and white columns of varying heights by **Daniel Buren** are a striking example of contemporary art in an historic setting. The central façade overlooking the square is decorated with allegorical statues. Beyond the double colonnaded Orléans Gallery is the garden. Built during the Restoration

(1814–30), the gallery was once covered by an iron and glass roof.

Jardin du Palais-Royal★★ *see Parks and Gardens.*

Le Louvre des Antiquaires – *Rue Saint-Honoré. 01 42 97 27 27. www.louvre-antiquaires.com. Open Tue–Sun.* A vast treasure trove of beautiful antiques in a building containing some 250 stores and stalls.

Place André-Malraux★ – Glance up the avenue de l'Opéra for another of those vistas that Paris does so well. The square was named after De Gaulle's minister of culture.

Galerie Véro-Dodat – *Rue Croix des Petits Champs.* A charming covered shopping passage. It was created in 1826 in a Neoclassical style by two butchers, Vero and Dodat, and was one of the first streets to feature gas lamps.

Comédie-Française – *2 rue Richelieu.* Attending a performance is the best way to appreciate this fine theater. In the foyer is a bust of **Voltaire★★** by Jean-Antoine Houdon and the chair in which Molière was sitting when he was taken fatally ill on stage in a performance of *Le Malade imaginaire* in 1673.

Rue de Richelieu – **Molière** lived at **no. 40**. Outside is the 19C **fountain** designed in his memory by Visconti, with statues by Jean-Jacques Pradier. **Stendhal** wrote his novels *Le Rouge at le Noir* and *Promenades dans Rome* at **no. 61**.

Rue Ste Anne – The façade of **no. 47** is decorated with music motifs and masks. It was the house of composer Jean-Baptiste Lully who borrowed money from Molière to have it built in 1671.

Rue de l'Échelle – "L'Échelle" refers to the ladder or flight of steps that led to a scaffold standing on this site in the *Ancien Régime*. It was used to humiliate polygamists, perjurers, and blasphemers.

Tour 2 – Place des Victoires
See map p 45.
✕ **Lunch stop** – Galerie Vivienne, Arcades.

Place des Victoires★ – The equestrian statue of Louis XIV was made by Bosio in 1822 to replace the original statue of the king, which was melted down in 1792.

Rue du Mail – Take a look at **nos. 5 and 7**, where carvings of a faun's mask and cornucopias adorn one doorway and the capitals of the other are interlaced with grass snakes, the emblem of Louis XIV's minister Jean-Baptiste Colbert.

Basilique de Notre-Dame-des-Victoires – *Place des Petits-Pères. 01 42 60 90 47. www.notre damedesvictoires.com. Open Mon–Sat 7.30am–7.45pm, Sun 8.30am–7.45pm.* Louis XIII commenced the building of the basilica in honor of his military victories in 1829, and it served as the chapel for the Petits-Pères monastery. In 1795–1809 it housed the Stock Exchange.

The Arcades – *5 rue de la Banque.* Built in 1823, the **Galerie Vivienne** is one of the prettiest arcades in Paris, with mosaics designed by Italian artist Facchina. On the mezzanine floor there are half-moon windows, and light floods in through the glass roof. It is lined with fashion boutiques and interesting old bookshops. There is also a tearoom if you feel in need of some refreshment. The **Galerie Colbert** is now part of the Bibliothèque Française.

Bibliothèque nationale de France: site Richelieu – *58 rue Vivienne. www.bnf.fr. Exhibitions open Tue–Sat 10am–7pm, Sun noon–7pm. Closed public holidays, 2 weeks in September. 9€.* The national library was founded with the collection of François I and has received a copy of every book published in France since. The Richelieu site holds specialized collections of ancient manuscripts. The **Mazarin Gallery★** and **Medals and Antiques Museum★** are also housed here.

Rue des Petits-Champs – Look through the grille at **no. 8** to see the courtyard and façade of the Hôtel Tubeuf (1648–55). Turn right into another covered 19C arcade, **Passage Choiseul**. It fell out of favor but enjoyed a new lease of life in the 1970s when fashion designer Kenzo opened a shop here, though the couturier has now moved elsewhere.

La Bourse (Stock Exchange) – *Place de la Bourse.* Founded in 1724 and sited first in Palais Mazarin (now part of the Bibliothèque Nationale) and then in the church of Notre-Dame-des-Victoires. Napoléon commissioned this building in 1808.

Tour 3 – Around rue de Rivoli

✕ **Lunch stop** – Rue Royale.

Place des Pyramides – It was here that **Joan of Arc** was wounded on September 8, 1429 when leading her attack on Paris. Her equestrian statue is by the 19C sculptor, Emmanuel Frémiet.

Rue de Rivoli★ – Now a major shopping street, rue de Rivoli has witnessed two major historic events: the proclamation of the Republic on September 21, 1792, and the arrest of General von Choltitz in August 1944.

Rue St-Honoré★ – Before rue de Rivoli was made, this road was the main route west out of Paris, and it was where the nobility and financiers shopped. In 1794 the tumbril carrying Robespierre to the guillotine paused in front of **no. 398** where he had lodged. Today it's the fashion stores that impress and catch the eye.

Église St-Roch★ – *296 rue St-Honoré. 01 42 44 13 20. http:// saintrochparis.cef.fr. Open daily 8am–7pm.* In 1795 the church was the scene of fierce fighting, when a young General Bonaparte gave orders for the protestors massed on the church steps to be fired upon. The bullet holes can still be seen.

Le Louvre★★★ *see Major Museums*
Jardin des Tuileries★ *see Parks and Gardens*
Musée des Arts décoratifs★★ *see Major Museums*

Musée de la Mode et du Textile★ – *107 rue de Rivoli. 01 44 55 57 50. www.lesartsdecoratifs.fr. Open Tue–Fri 11am–6pm, Sat–Sun 10am–6pm. Closed public holidays. 8€.* There are more than 20,000 outfits and 21,000 fabric samples in the Museum of Textiles and Fashion. All the big couturiers have work here, including Christian Dior and Elsa Schiaparelli, while textile exhibits include those designed by Raoul Dufy and Sonia Delaunay.

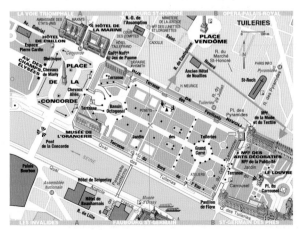

PARIS CENTER

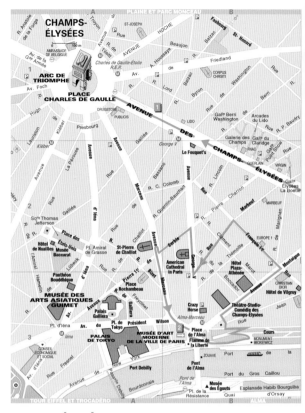

CHAMPS-ÉLYSÉES★★★

The most famous street in Paris ends in a blaze of glory at the Arc de Triomphe. The surrounding area is smart and classically French. Everything has an air of grandeur from the luxury stores and car showrooms, to the cinemas, where premieres are held and the public buildings such as the Grand Palais. Much of the area bears the stamp of Baron Haussmann, who, more than anyone else, is responsible for the way Paris looks today. His vision was to create a well-ordered, airy city.

Tour 1 – Walking up the Champs-Élysées

Ⓜ *Concorde (lines 1, 8, and 12). Buses: 22, 28, 31, 42, 52, 73, 83, 84, 92, 94.*

✕ **Lunch stop** – Avenue des Champs-Élysées.

Place de la Concorde★★★ – *See Landmarks.*

Two mansions★★ – Before making your way up the Champs-Élysées pause to look at the imposing mansions on either side of the entrance to rue Royale.

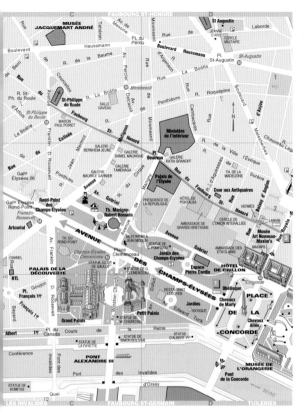

They are the finest architectural examples of the Louis XVI style. The **Hôtel de Crillon** now houses the French Automobile Club.

Musée de l'Orangerie★★
see Great Galleries

The Gardens★ – Landscaped with trees, look out for the statues of statesmen such as Clemenceau, De Gaulle, and Churchill, and leader of the Resistance Jean Moulin.

Avenue des Champs-Élysées★★★ – Most of the 19C houses and amusement halls that once lined this road have been replaced by international retailers and restaurants. The exception is the former home of La Païva, a Polish adventuress, at **no. 25**. It became renowned for the dinners attended by writers, philosophers, and painters. Along the side roads are luxury fashion stores and boutiques.

Arc de Triomphe★★★
see Landmarks

49

Tour 2 – Round tour from place de l'Alma

Ⓜ *Alma-Marceau or Iéna (line 9).*
Buses: 63, 72, 80, 92.
See map pp 48–49.
✕ **Lunch stop** – Rue François 1er.

Place de l'Alma – A life-sized model of the flame held by New York's Statue of Liberty has become an unofficial memorial to Diana, Princess of Wales, who died after a crash in the nearby tunnel.

Pont de l'Alma – The asymmetical steel bridge has a span of 361ft/110m. When reconstructed in the early 1970s, three of the four statues of soldiers that had decorated it were removed and only the **zouave** now remains. Parisians use him as a highwater mark when the Seine swells to dangerous levels.

Cours Albert-1er – In these pleasant gardens alongside the Seine is a statue of the Polish poet **Mickiewicz** by Antoine Bourdelle. At **no. 40** you will also see a fine façade by Réne Lalique.

Zouave stands below the Pont de l'Alma
© S. Sauvignier / MICHELIN

Avenue Montaigne – The elegant buildings, luxury fashion stores, and art galleries exude an atmosphere of wealth and style that are the antithesis of the era in the 19C when the main attraction was the Mabille Dance Hall.

Théâtre des Champs-Élysées – This theater was one of the first major monuments to be built in reinforced concrete in 1912. Bourdelle designed the statues on the façade. Inside, the ceiling painted by **Maurice Denis** sets the scene for dramatic appearances made at the theater from Stravinsky's *Rite of Spring* and **Diaghilev**, to **Jean Cocteau** and **Josephine Baker**.

Rue Bayard – You can't miss **no. 22**, the home of RTL, Radio-Télé-Luxembourg, decorated by Victor Vasarely.

Avenue George-V – Famous for the grand hotel of the same name, the **American Cathedral in Paris** is also located here, as is the famous **Crazy-Horse** music hall.

Église St-Pierre-de-Chaillot – *35 ave Marceau. 01 47 20 12 33. Open Mon–Sat 7.30am–1pm, 3–7pm, Sun 7.30–noon, 5–8.15pm.* Rebuilt in 1937 in the neo-Romanesque style, the church has a belfry 213ft/65m high. On the façade of the church is a striking carving by Bouchard of the Life of St Peter.

Musée des Égouts *see For Kids*
Musée national des Arts asiatiques★★★ – Guimet *see Major Museums*

Tour 3 – Along rue du Faubourg Saint-Honoré★

Ⓜ *Concorde (lines 1, 8, and 12).*
Buses: 24, 42, 52, 80, 84, 94.
See map pp 48–49.
✕ **Lunch stop** – Boulevard des Capucines.

Rue du Faubourg-St-Honoré★ – Starting at rue Royale, this street is full of luxury boutiques, art galleries, and fine mansions. You may notice too there is not a no. 13 here—the legacy of the superstitious Empress Eugénie.

Palais de l'Élysée – *55 rue du Faubourg-St-Honoré. Closed to public.* Built in 1718 for the Count of Évreux, since 1873 the Palais has been the home of the French president. **Napoléon III** lived here too when he was planning his successful *coup d'etat* of 1851.

Place Beauvau – The 18C mansion built for the Prince of Beauvau-Craon is now home to the Ministry of Home Affairs.

Avenue de Marigny – The former Hôtel de Rothschild and its park at **no. 23** are now used for official visiting dignitaries. The Théâtre Marigny is in the garden of the Champs Élysées.

Maison Paul Poiret

The couturier Paul Poiret (1879–1944) was based at no. 107 rue du Faubourg-St-Honoré. He banned the whale-bone corset and inspired a trend for theatrical styles, strong colors, and exotic dress design. Ankle-length hobble skirts and Japanese kimono-style sleeves are just two of his influential designs.

Avenue Matignon – This street is lined with art galleries. English auctioneer Christie's is housed at **no. 9** in a mansion designed by René Sergent in 1913.

Rue du Colisée – The road was named after a Roman-style theater that could seat 40,000 spectators. It was built in 1770 by Le Camus.

Église St-Philippe-du-Roule – *154 rue du Faubourg-St-Honoré. 01 53 53 00 44. www.stphilippedu roule.org. Open Mon–Fri 7.30am–6pm (Wed 7pm, Thu 6.45pm), Sun 9am–12.30pm, 3.45–7.45pm.* Designed by **Chalgrin**, architect of the Arc de Triomphe, in the style of a Roman Basilica, the church was built between 1774 and 1784. The fresco of *The Deposition* was painted by Théodore Chassérieu.

Rue du Faubourg-St-Honoré

Photographer: Marc Bertrand

PARIS CENTER

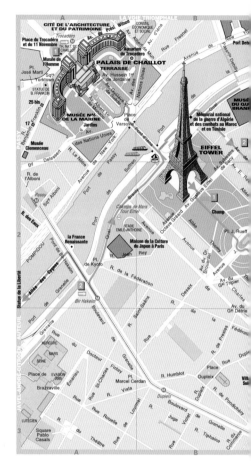

TROCADÉRO★★

Taking its name from the Place du Trocadéro, this is an imposing area of wide open spaces and monumental buildings. Looking over to the Left Bank of the Seine— you can't miss the Eiffel Tower opposite.

Tour 1 – From the Trocadéro to Maison de l' UNESCO

Ⓜ *Trocadéro (lines 6 and 9).*
Buses: 22, 30, 32, 63, 82.
✕ **Lunch stop** – Place du Trocadéro et du 11-Novembre.

Place du Trocadéro et du 11-Novembre –The roads radiate out across Paris from beneath the stern gaze of the equestrian statue of Marshal Foch, commander of Allied forces during World War I.

the **Cité de l'Architecture et du Patrimoine★★** are both located in the palace, and set out in front are the **Trocadéro Gardens★★★**, created for the 1937 Exhibition.

Pont d'Iéna – From place de Varsovie cross the Seine by the pont d'Iéna.

Eiffel Tower★★★
see Landmarks

Champs de Mars – Once used for military parades and exhibitions, this is now a vast formal garden. Look for **The Wall for Peace** near the Eiffel Tower, it was erected in 2000.

Village suisse – On the site of a Swiss village in the 1900 World's Fair, the area is known for its antiques shops.

École Militaire★ – *1 place Joffre.* Louis XV built a Royal Military Academy in the 1750s to train as officers young men without the financial means necessary. A 15-year-old Bonaparte was sworn in as a cadet in 1784 and graduated in record time. Today it still functions as a military academy and study institute.

Maison de l'UNESCO★ – *7 place de Fontenoy. 01 45 68 16 42.* Opened in 1958, the HQ of the United Nations Educational, Scientific, and Cultural Organization was designed by international architects, highlighting UNESCO's strong spirit of cooperation. A statue by Henry Moore, *Figure in Repose*, can be seen from avenue de Suffren.

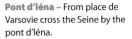

Palais de Chaillot★★ – Built in 1939, the spectacular palace consists of twin curved pavilions linked by a central portico. From the broad terrace there's a stunning **view★★★** of the Seine, the Eiffel Tower, and École Militaire. Below the palace is the **Théâtre national de Chaillot**, one of the largest theaters in Paris. The **Musée de l'Homme★★** and

53

Musée du Quai Branly with the tip of the Eiffel Tower

© Bruno Bernier / Fotolia.com

Tour 2 – Along the Seine and around the Tower

Ⓜ *Bir-Hakeim (line 6). RER: Champs-de-Mars-Tour-Eiffel (line C). Buses: 82, 92.*
See map pp 52–53.
✕ **Lunch stop** – Boulevard de Grenelle.

Allée des Cygnes – Before you start, take a quick detour to this small artificial island in the Seine, halfway across Bir Hakeim bridge. From here you will have a good view of the **Maison de Radio-France★** *(see p 55)* and the bronze replica of the **Statue of Liberty**.

Musée du quai Branly★★ – *37 quai Branly. 01 56 61 70 00. www.quaibranly.fr. Open Tue–Sun 11am–7pm (Thu–Sat 9pm). 9€.* Dedicated to the art and cultures of Africa, Asia, Oceania, and the Americas, this museum opened in 2006 has a wealth of fascinating exhibits. Outside is equally worth a peek with an extraordinary "living wall" of vegetation. Enjoy a view of the museum gardens from the terrace of the upscale Restaurant Les Ombres.

Avenue Rapp – From quai Branly turn first into ave de la Bourdonnais, then into rue Général Camou, which leads to **no. 29** ave Rapp. Created in the Art Nouveau style by Jules Lavirotte in 1901, it has an elaborate ceramic façade. Lavirotte's own home, also in Art Nouveau style, is at **no. 3**.

Rue St-Dominique – Take a detour to no. 129 to see François-Jean Bralle's **Fontaine de Mars**.

Avenue de la Bourdonnais – Returning to ave de la Bourdonnais, approach place de l'École Militaire. At rue du Champ-de-Mars visit **no. 33** to see a fine floral façade design by Racine in 1900.

PASSY

Ⓜ *Passy (line 6). RER: Kennedy-Radio France (line C). Buses: 22, 32, 52, PC.*

Cimetière de Passy – *2 rue du Commandant-Schloesing. 01 43 28 47 63. Open Sat 8am–5.30pm, Sun 9am–5.30pm. Guided tours Sat (2hr). 6€.* You will find the graves of the rich and famous here, including the composer Claude Debussy, painter Edouard Manet, not to mention the odd count and princess. Gordon Bennett, publisher of the *New York Herald*, is also buried in the cemetery.

Musée du Vin, Caveau des Échansons – 5–7 square Charles-Dickens. 01 45 25 63 26. www. museeduvinparis.com. Open Tue–Sun 10am–6pm. Closed Dec 25, Jan 1. Entry with glass of wine 11.90€. With France's reputation for wine still going strong, it is only natural to find a museum dedicated to wine in Paris. Set in the site of an old quarry (**no. 5 rue des Eaux** marks the original quarry entrance) there are exhibits on everything to do with wine, with mannequins and equipment.

Rue de l'Annonciation – Take a chance to browse the shops, relax in a café, or look inside the 17C **Eglise Notre-Dame-de-Grâce-de-Passy**. There are a number of exclusive and luxury stores in the rue de Passy.

Rue Berton – A narrow street with ivy-clad houses and old-fashioned gas lamps. Make your way to **no. 24** to imagine Balzac sneaking out of here from the back entrance of his home in order to escape his creditors, as he is said to have done.

Rue Raynouard – As befits this wealthy residential area, a number of influential people have lived here, including American tycoon William Kissam Vanderbilt. Other famous inhabitants include **Benjamin Franklin** at no. 66 and **Jean-**

Jacques Rousseau. The writer **Honoré de Balzac** lived at no. 47. His cottage is now a museum.

AUTEUIL
Ⓜ *Église-d'Auteuil, Michel-Ange-d'Auteuil (line 10). Buses: 32, 52, 70 for Maison de Radio-France.*

Maison de Radio-France★ – 116 avenue du Président-Kennedy. Museum: 01 56 40 15 16. Museum closed for renovations. The distinctive concentric home of Radio France. Live music performances are open to the public.

Fondation Le Corbusier – 8–10 square du Dr-Blanche. 01 42 88 41 53. www.fondationlecorbusier. asso. fr. Open Tue–Sat 10am–6pm. Closed 1st week in Aug and public holidays. 8€. A museum of the work of the ground-breaking modernist architect Charles Édouard Jeanneret—known as Le Corbusier. It holds thousands of original drawings, studies, and plans, and has an extensive photographic archive.

A village in Paris
The last vineyards disappeared from Auteil at the turn of the 19C, and it became part of Paris in 1859, but this very select *quartier* still enjoys something of a village atmosphere today. Note the villas in **rue Molitor**, **rue Boileau**, and **rue Jouvenet**. You'll see houses by Art Nouveau architect Hector Guimard, with fine examples in **rue La-Fontaine** and **rue Agar**. He is famous for his ornate entrances to the Paris Métro.

BEAUBOURG★★ AND LES HALLES

As elsewhere in Paris, the old and the new are jumbled up together in this historic district, but it is the new that leaves the overriding impression, perhaps because, as in the case of the Beaubourg, the architecture is so striking.

Tour 1 – St Merri Quarter

Ⓜ *Châtelet (lines 1, 4, 7, 11, 14).*
RER: Châtelet-les Halles.
Buses: 29, 38, 47.
✕ **Lunch stop** – Rue St-Merri.

Rue Quincampoix – Scottish financier John Law famously founded a bank here in 1719, and set in train the South Sea Bubble. Speculators gathered in this street, making vast fortunes until 1720 when the bank crashed and they fled. Today, among the stylish galleries, stores, and bars are some old houses at **nos. 10–14**, which are notable for their unusual paved courtyards, carved doors, stone masks, and wrought-iron balconies.

Église St-Merri★ – *Access to the church via rue St-Martin or the St Merri presbytery (76 rue de la Verrerie). 01 42 71 93 93. www.saint merri.org. Open daily 11am–7pm.* Hemmed into the narrow street alongside small houses and stores, the church appears much as it must have done when built in the 16C. Inside is a fine 17C organ loft and beautiful wood paneling on the pulpit and sacristy by the Slodtz brothers. One of the bells dates from 1331, from the medieval chapel that previously stood on the site, and is thought to be the oldest in Paris.

Place Stravinsky – The **Stravinski Fountain★** is one of the most entertaining and photographed in Paris. A far cry from the classic elegance of Visconti's fountains, it was designed by **Jean Tinguely** and **Niki de Saint Phalle** in 1983 and features eyecatching kinetic sculptures.

Rue St-Merri – Take a detour to see the interesting façades on **nos. 9 and 12**. Just a few steps farther is **impasse du Bœuf**, one of the oldest cul-de-sacs in Paris.

Plateau Beaubourg – Place Georges Pompidou – When plans for the major redevelopment of the area known as the Plateau Beaubourg were first

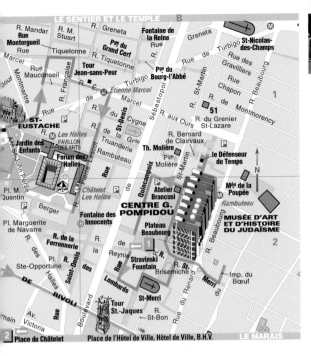

R. Mandar · **Rue Montorgueil** · R. M. Stuart · R. Greneta · **Fontaine de la Reine** · Greneta · Turbigo · **St-Nicolas-des-Champs**

Rue · Tiquetonne · Pge du **Grand Cerf** · Rue · de · Rue des Gravilliers

Marcel · Rue Mauconseil · R. Française · R. Tiquetonne · **Tour Jean-sans-Peur** · Turbigo · Rue · St-Martin · Rue Chapon · Beaubourg

Jour · Rue · de · Étienne Marcel · Pge du **Bourg-l'Abbé** · R. de · Montmorency

Montmartre · Rue · Marcel · R. du Cygne · Sébastopol · R. aux Ours · **51** · R. du Grenier St-Lazare

ST-EUSTACHE · Les Halles · PAVILLON DES ARTS · R. de la Grde Truanderie · R. Bernard de Clairvaux · **Th. Molière** · **le Défenseur du Temps**

Jardin des Enfants · **Forum des Halles** · Rambuteau · Pge Molière · St-Martin · **Mée de la Poupée** · N

St-John Perse · Pierre · Lescot · Châtelet Les Halles · de · Quincampoix · **Atelier Brancusi** · Rambuteau

Pl. M. Quentin · Berger · **CENTRE G. POMPIDOU** · **MUSÉE D'ART ET D'HISTOIRE DU JUDAÏSME**

Pl. Marguerite de Navarre · **Fontaine des Innocents** · **Plateau Beaubourg** · R. Beaubourg · 2

R. de la Ferronerie · R. de la Reynie · **1** · **Stravinski Fountain** · R. St-Brisemiche · **Merri** · Imp. du Bœuf

Pl. Ste-Opportune · Saint-Denis · des · Rue · **Lombards** · R. du Renard · du

DE RIVOLI · Boulevard · **Tour St.-Jaques** · **St-Merri** · St-Bon

main · Av. Victoria · Rue

mooted, a public library was to be built. However, in 1969 French president **Georges Pompidou** opted for a multipurpose cultural center instead. In fine weather, people gather in the square, strumming guitars and chatting, or watching performances by the area's many street entertainers.

Centre Georges-Pompidou★★★ – *Rue Croix des Petits Champs, place Georges Pompidou. 01 44 78 12 33. www.centrepompidou.fr. Open Wed–Sun 11am–10pm. Closed May 1.* **Richard Rogers** and **Renzo Piano** completed this unique "inside-out" building (also known as the Beaubourg) in 1977. The colored pipes on the exterior of the build-ing are functional, carrying water, electrical cables, and ventilation shafts. An escalator also climbs up the outside of the building, visible through a large transpar-ent tube. As well as the **Musée national d'Art moderne★★★**, it also houses the **Bibliothèque publique d'information** and **IRCAM** (the Institute for Accoustic and Musical Research).

Musée national d'Art moderne★★★ *see Great Galleries*

Quartier de l'Horloge – **Le Défenseur du Temps** (The Defender of Time) features a life-size figure who battles animals symbolizing the elements as the hours strike. A dragon represents Earth, a bird air, and a crab water.

57

Place du Châtelet

© S. Sauvignier / MICHELIN

Tour 2 – Around Châtelet-Hôtel de Ville★

Ⓜ *Châtelet (lines 1, 4, 7, 11, and 14), Hôtel-de-Ville (lines 1 and 11). RER: Châtelet (lines A, B, and D). Buses: 21, 69, 70, 72, 74, 75, 76, 81, 96. See map pp 56–57.*
✕ **Lunch stop** – Place du Châtelet.

Place du Châtelet – Named after the great fortress that guarded the northern entrance into the city, over the Pont au Change. The **Palm Tree Fountain**, in the center of the square, celebrates Napoléon's many victories.

Quai de la Mégisserie – The fine **view★★** extending over the law courts, Conciergerie, and the river belies this area's past when slaughterhouses lined the river banks.

Église St-Germain-l'Auxerrois★★ – *2 quai du Louvre. 01 42 60 13 96. www.saintgermain auxerrois.cef.fr. Open daily 8am–7pm.* The church, built over five centuries, has particular significance for the St Bartholomew's Day Massacre of the Huguenots on August 24, 1572. When the bells rang for matins they signaled the beginning of the bloodshed.

Tour St-Jacques★ – *39 rue de Rivoli. www.tour-saint-jacques-par-is.com. Not currently open for visits.* Now a weather station, the tower is the former belfry of St-Jacques-la-Boucherie, which was a starting point for pilgrimages to Santiago de Compostela in Spain.

Place de l'Hôtel-de-Ville – Known as place de Grève until 1830, in the Middle Ages it was a meeting place for those out of work. It was also the gruesome site of public executions during the Ancien Règime.

Hôtel de Ville★ – *29 rue de Rivoli. 01 42 76 50 49. www.paris.fr/english/visit/heritage-and-sights/p8221. Open Sat by appointment.* Entirely rebuilt between 1874 and 1882, following the fire during the fall of the Paris Commune in 1871, the Hôtel de Ville (city hall) has played a major part in French history. Throughout the Revolution it was controlled by the Commune, and it was the site from which the Second and Third Republics were proclaimed on February 24, 1848 and September 4, 1870. General de Gaulle also made his famous speech here on August 25, 1944 following the liberation of Paris. It now houses the mayor of Paris and the city's administrative offices.

B.H.V. (Bazar de l'Hôtel de Ville) – A store dating from the 1850s. *See Shopping.*

Pont Notre-Dame – This bridge was on the royal route into Paris, when it was lined with richly decorated houses.

Pont au Change – The name derives from the moneychangers who set up their stalls here in the Middle Ages.

Tour 3 – Around Les Halles

Ⓜ *Les Halles (line 4). RER: Châtelet (lines A, B, and D). Buses: 29, 38, 47. See map pp 56–57.*

✕ **Lunch stop** – Rue Montorgueil.

La Bourse du Commerce – *2 rue de Viarmes.* This circular building, lit by a vast glass dome, was built as the Commodities Exchange in 1889. It is now used by the Paris Chamber of Commerce.

Jardin des Enfants – *see For Kids*

Église St-Eustache★★ – *Place du Jour. 01 42 36 31 05. www.saint-eustache.org. Open Mon–Fri 9.30am–7pm, Sat–Sun 9am–7pm.* The foundation stone for this stunning church, dedicated to a converted Roman general, was laid in 1532. It took over a century to build, however, and was only consecrated in 1640. The **north transept façade**★ has a fine Renaissance composition. St Eustache is depicted in the stained-glass windows in the

chancel. The organ is reputed to be the largest in France with an astounding 8,000 pipes. Louis XIV's minister of finance Jean-Baptiste Colbert is buried here.

Rue Montorgueil – A bustling street, lined with cafes and shops, quaint boutiques still exist here and in nearby rue Tiquetonne, rue Marie Stuart, and passage du Grand-Cerf.

Tour de Jean-sans-Peur – *20 rue Etienne Marcel. 01 40 26 20 28. www.tourjeansanspeur.com. Open Apr–Nov Wed–Sun 1.30–6pm; Nov–end Mar Wed, Sat, Sun 1.30–6pm. 5€.* Built by John the Fearless in 1409 after ordering the assassination of the Duke of Orléans, the interior reconstructs scenes from a medieval château.

Forum des Halles – *see Shopping*

Fontaine des Innocents★ – The square stands on the site of the 12C Holy Innocents church and cemetery. In 1786 the bones from the cemetery were transferred to the former quarries of La Tombe-Issoire which became the ossuary **Les Catacombes**★ *(see p 30).*

Forum des Halles

© S. Sauvignier / Michelin

PARIS BEYOND

Paris is such a neat, compact city that even those districts that are a little beyond the center are still within easy reach. Montmartre, Bastille, and the Opéra-Garnier are all just a short Métro ride away.

BASTILLE★

🅼 *Bastille (lines 1, 5, and 8).*
Buses: 20, 65, 69, 76, 86, 87, 91.
If there's one place in Paris that is symbolic of the historic revolution of 1789—and those of 1830 and 1848—it is the place de la Bastille, and it is still a potent rallying point for national celebrations. Originally famous for its dance halls, people now come to Bastille for the furniture workshops and artists' studios. The area around rue du Faubourg St-Antoine has been the heart of the cabinet-making industry in Paris for centuries, and still has a slightly nostalgic air about it—though it is also now well stocked with lively bars and cafés.

Tour – Around Bastille

✖ **Lunch stop** – Promenade Plantée.

Port de Plaisance de Paris-Arsenal – The pretty marina for privately owned boats that visit Paris was originally a moat for Charles V's fortified residence. It's now also a pleasant place to walk and relax or dine in one of the restaurants. From here the water

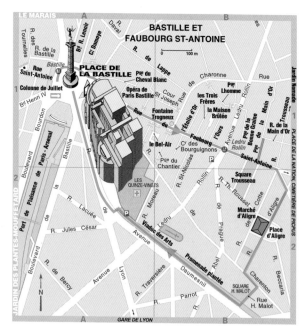

flows beneath the place de la Bastille and emerges further north as the **Canal St-Martin**★, which continues to the Bassin de La Villette in the north of Paris. For canal boat trips *see Sports and Activities*.

Place de la Bastille – The outline of the fortress-prison that was once here is marked out by special stones. It was famously stormed on July 14, 1789 and over the next months demolished entirely. The July column (171ft/52m) commemorates the Parisians killed in the 1830 and 1848 uprisings. The figure on top is the "Spirit of Freedom."

L'Opéra de Paris-Bastille★ *see Stage and Screen*

Rue du Faubourg St-Antoine – Browse the arcades and courtyards of this street lined with furniture stores, in particular **Passage de la Main-d'Or** (133 rue du Faubourg St-Antoine). On the corner with rue de Charonne is the **Fontaine Trogneux**, an old fountain dating from 1710.

Place d'Aligre *see Markets*

Viaduc des Arts★ – Once the route of the suburban railway to the Bastille, today the viaduct supports a lovely **Promenade Plantée**★ with trees and gardens. In the archways below are fine art and cabinet-making businesses.

Nearby

Cimetière de Picpus – *35 rue de Picpus. 01 43 44 18 54. Open Easter–Sept Tue–Sun 2–6pm; Oct–Easter Tue–Sun 2–4pm. 3€.* This cemetery was created around the communal graves of the victims of the guillotine. The French aristocrat who fought in the American Revolutionary War, the Marquis de Lafayette, is also buried here.

Église Ste-Marguerite – *36 rue St-Bernard. 01 43 71 34 24. Open Mon–Sat on request at the Acceuil.* Inside there's a marble *Pietà* behind the altar by Girardon and unusual 18C *trompe-l'œil* frescoes by Brunetti.

Place de la Nation – Visitors attracted by the more gruesome aspects of history, albeit at the safe distance of a couple of centuries, can imagine the dark days of the Revolution when a guillotine was erected here, which took 1,306 lives. The central sculpture, *The Triumph of the Republic*, was created for the first centenary of the Revolution.

PARIS BEYOND

🏛 MONTMARTRE★★★

With its colorful history as the *quartier* of choice for 19C and early 20C artists and composers such as Erik Satie, Toulouse Lautrec, and Picasso, there's still a whiff of decadence about Montmartre. The crowds come to absorb the atmosphere, see a cabaret, and enjoy a little nightlife.

Tour 1 – From boulevard de Rochechouart to Sacré-Cœur

Ⓜ *Anvers (line 2), Abbesses (line 12), Lamarck-Caulaincourt (line 12). Buses: 30, 54, 67, Montmartrobus.*
✕ **Lunch stop** – Rue des Abbesses.

Place Charles-Dullin – Save your feet by taking the funicular to the Sacré Cœur, or wind your way upward to explore the narrow back streets . Actor-director Charles Dullin opened the **Théâtre de l'Atelier** in this pretty square in 1922.

Martyrium – *11 rue Yvonne-Le-Tac.* A medieval sanctuary once marked the site where St Denis is said to have been decapitated. **Ignatius Loyola** founded the Jesuit Order here on August 15, 1534.

Place des Abbesses★ – The heart of Montmartre and the base of the butte (hill) of Montmartre. Look for the beautiful Art Nouveau entrance to the Métro station by Hector Guimard. It is just one of two remaining in Paris.

Église St-Jean-de-Montmartre – *place des Abbesses.* This church is unsual for its early use of reinforced concrete, which forms the structure, clad with brick. It was designed by Baudot in 1904.

Place Émile-Goudeau★ – Forever identified with the modernist painters and poets who flocked here from the 1900s and occupied **Le Bateau-Lavoir** studios. Among the artists were

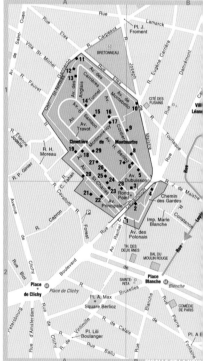

Braque, Van Dongen, and Picasso, who painted Les *Demoiselles d'Avignon* here, while Max Jacob, Apollinaire, and Mac Orlan numbered among the poets. By the time World War I broke out in 1914, the bohemians and artists had started to move away, many to Montparnasse nearer the center of the city.

Carrefour de l'Auberge de la Bonne-Franquette – In the late 19C Émile Zola and the painters Pissarro, Sisley, Cézanne, Toulouse-Lautrec, Renoir, and Monet congregated in this area. Maurice Utrillo also painted here in the 20C.

Place du Tertre★★ – Early in the morning this shaded square could be in a peaceful village, yet by noon it is a lively tourist attraction, packed with visitors in the busy restaurants, and street artists.

Église St Pierre-de-Montmartre★ – *2 rue du Mont-Cenis.* The church of Saint Peter is the last surviving vestige of the great abbey of Montmartre and one of the oldest churches in Paris, dating back to 1134. Yet it has been restored and added to over the centuries. The three bronze doors showing St Denis, St Peter, and the Virgin were made by

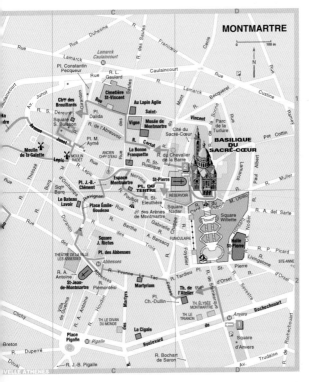

MONTMARTRE

BASILIQUE DU SACRÉ-CŒUR

the Italian sculptor, Tommaso Gismondi, in 1980.

Basilique du Sacré-Cœur★★
see Landmarks

Tour 2 – From Sacré-Cœur to Moulin Rouge

Ⓜ *Anvers (line 2), Abbesses (line 12), Lamarck-Caulaincourt (line 12). Buses: 30, 54, 67, Montmartrobus. See map pp 62–63.*
✕ **Lunch stop** – Rue Lepic.

Rue Cortot – Immortalized in a painting by Renoir, rue Cortot is said to have counted Renoir, Dufy, and Utrillo—and the radical poet Pierre Reverdy—among its inhabitants at **no.12**, now a museum.

Musée de Montmartre – *12 rue Cortot. 01 49 25 89 37. www.museedemontmartre.fr. Open daily 10am–6pm. 9€.* The Musée de Montmartre houses a fascinating collection of mementoes from the 12C through the quarter's Bohemian days, to its 20C nightclubs and personalities. The Jardins Renoir offer a bucolic view over the local vineyards.

Clos du Montmartre vineyard (Le Vigne) – Don't miss the quaint houses around the vineyard of this once prominent wine-producing area. The grapes are harvested for the Clos du Montmartre wine on the first Saturday in October.

Rue St-Vincent – At the junction of rue St-Vincent with **rue des Saules** is one of the most interesting corners of the district—a flight of stairs drops

away abruptly and the road rises steeply beside the **cemetery**. On the corner is the famous **Lapin Agile**. **Hector Berlioz** lived at the junction with **rue du Mont-Cenis**, where he composed *Harold in Italy* and *Benvenuto Cellini*.

Lapin Agile – *22 rue des Saules. 01 46 06 85 87. www.au-lapin-agile.com. Open Tue–Sun 9pm–1am. 28€.* In the 1900s this cabaret and restaurant attracted many often penniless writers and artists. It is still a popular venue today offering traditional French songs, dance, and comedy. *See Nightlife.*

Lapin Agile Café-Théâtre

© Ilpo Musto / APA Publications

Cimetière St-Vincent – Among the people buried in this small cemetery are the composer Honegger, the painter Utrillo, the writer Marcel Aymé, and singer Émile Goudeau.

Château des Brouillards – Built as a folly in the 18C, the château was later used as a dance hall. Its grounds were turned into square Suzanne-Buisson, named after the French resistance fighter who was killed in World War II. A statue of St Denis stands on the spot where he is said to have washed his decapitated head.

Avenue Junot – A peaceful road with artists' studios alongside private houses, including the **Hameau des Artistes** (no. 11) and the **Villa Léandre**★ (no. 25). From no. 10 there is a view of the Moulin de la Galette restaurant.

Moulin de la Galette – The open-air dance hall and café that were here in the late 19C attracted and inspired many painters, including Renoir and Van Gogh. The windmill itself, the Blute-fin, has topped the hill for more than six centuries. During the siege of Paris in 1814 its owner, Pierre-Charles Debray, defended it against the Cossacks. His corpse was finally crucified upon the sails.

Rue Lepic – **Van Gogh** lived with his brother, Theo, for a time at **no. 54** of this road which winds its way down a steep hill. A veteran car rally takes place here each fall.

Cimetière de Montmartre – *20 Avenue Rachel. 01 53 42 36 30. Guided tours by appointment.* As a detour, you could explore Montmartre cemetery, the final resting place of many famous people, including the dramatist Labiche, painter Edgar Degas, the great dancer Nijinsky, actor Louis Jouvet, composer Jacques Offenbach, and film director François Truffaut.

Place Blanche – Rue Lepic leads to place Blanche and the cabarets, bars, and nightclubs of Pigalle.

Moulin Rouge – *82 blvd de Clichy. 01 53 09 82 82. www. moulinrouge.fr. Shows daily 9pm and 11pm.* The Moulin Rouge,

the most famous of the Parisian dance halls, opened its doors in 1889 with the Cancan star Louise Weber, and came to symbolize the *belle époque*. Dance shows are still staged daily.

PIGALLE
Ⓜ *Place de Clichy (lines 2 and 13), Pigalle (lines 2 and 12), Blanche (line 2). Buses: 30, 54, 67.*

Boulevard de Clichy – With its restaurants, cinemas, theaters, and nightclubs, the area around the boulevard and square is a hub for Paris nightlife.

Boulevard de Rochechouart – Busy with cosmopolitan clubs and bars, the only remnant of the old dance halls and cabarets such as La Boule Noire (1822) and Le Chat Noir (1881) is the Élysée Montmartre music venue at **no. 72**.

Musée de la Vie Romantique – *16 rue Chaptal. 01 53 31 95 67. www.vie-romantique.paris.fr. Open Tue–Sun 10am–6pm. No charge for permanent collection.* Set in the home of the painter **Ary Scheffer** (1795–1858), the museum gives an atmospheric window onto both his life and that of **George Sand**.

Musée de la Vie Romantique

© Paris Tourist Office – Photographer: Amélie Dupont

PARIS BEYOND

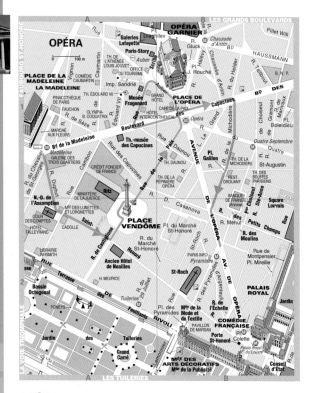

OPÉRA★★
AND LES GRANDS
BOULEVARDS★

A district of broad avenues and imposing buildings, the Opéra-Garnier forms the focal point and is the epitome of *belle époque* style and grandeur. The boulevards may no longer be filled with gentlemen in top hats arm-in-arm with elegant companions, but the presence of the *grands magasins*—big department stores such as Galeries Lafayettes—ensures the area is always buzzing.

Tour – Around the Opéra★★

Ⓜ *Madeleine (lines 8, 12, and 14).*
Buses: 24, 42, 52, 84, 94.
✕**Lunch stop** – Place de l'Opéra.

La Madeleine★★ – *place de la Madeleine. 01 44 51 69 17. www. eglise-lamadeleine.com. Open daily 9.30am–7pm.* Built in the Neoclassical style, this church dedicated to St Mary Magdalene is surrounded by 52 Corinthian columns. The pediment has a sculpted relief of the Last Judgment. Inside there is a single nave with **three domes**. Behind the altar a huge statue by

Charles Marochetti depicts Mary Magdalene being transported to heaven by two angels.

Place de la Madeleine – Among the fashion stores and flower market are the renowned Fauchon and Hédiard, the term *épicerie* (grocer) scarcely does them justice.

Place Vendôme★★ – Named after the illegitimate son of Henri IV, the square is a perfect example of French 17C design. **Coco Chanel** lived here for many years while she ran her fashion empire in a house in rue Cambon nearby. The statue that stands on top of the tall central column is of Napoléon.

Rue de la Paix – A street lined with highly exclusive and fashionable shops, including a number of upscale jewelers.

Place de l'Opéra★★ – Georges Eugène Haussmann created this square as another circus from which grand roads could radiate into the city. Today it is lined with luxury stores and cafés and is one of the city's busiest intersections.

Boulevard des Capucines – Named after a Capuchin convent on the site, note the fine Art Nouveau styling at **no. 27**.

Rue Scribe – Take a detour to see the very aptly named Grand Hotel, built in the elegant Empire style of Napoléon III.

L'Opéra-Garnier★★ *see Landmarks*

Place Gaillion – Erected in 1707, the beautiful fountain in the square was remodeled by Louis Visconti in 1827.

Avenue de l'Opéra – Haussmann completed this grand avenue in 1878. Unusually for Paris it has no trees, the result of Charles Garnier's desire for an uninterrupted view to his opera house.

Les Grands Boulevards★
M *Richelieu Drouot (lines 8 and 9), Strasbourg-St Denis (lines 4, 8, and 9), Grands Boulevards (lines 8 and 9). Buses: 20, 38, 39, 47, 48.*

Boulevard des Italiens – Built by Haussman as part of his transformation of this area in the 19C, it was named after the popular acting troupe for the Opéra-Comique.Today cinemas draw the crowd.

Boulevard Montmartre – A very lively road. **No. 47** still has its old-fashioned frontage. Passage Jouffroy at **no. 10** contains an interesting hotchpotch of shops, while the Passage des Panoramas was opened in 1799 at **no. 11**.

Porte St-Denis★ and Porte St-Martin★ – The imposing gates were built in the 1670s to celebrate military victories by Louis XIV. The kings of France would pass under Port St-Denis after attending mass at the Basilica at Saint Denis. This gate is said to be the inspiration for the **Arc de Triomphe★★★** *(see Landmarks)*. The Porte St-Martin replaced a medieval gate.

Musée Grévin★, Les Étoiles du Rex *see For Kids*

Stars of Belleville

Myth surrounds the birth of Giovanna Gassion, who became singer **Édith Piaf**, but what is certain is that she was born in abject poverty. Discovered by a nightclub owner singing in the streets of Belleville and Pigalle, Édith went on to become world famous with strong and passionate renditions of songs such as *La Vie en Rose* and *Je Ne Regrette Rien*. The small private **Musée Édith Piaf** at 5 rue Crespin du Gast near Ménilmontant Métro station is dedicated to her memory. Another famous entertainer to come from this area was **Maurice Chevalier**. Before achieving Hollywood fame he was known for songs that were rooted in Belleville such as *Ma Pomme* and *Marche de Ménilmontant*.

BELLEVILLE★

Ⓜ *Belleville (lines 2 and 11), Pyrénées (line 11), Ménilmontant (line 2), Gambetta (lines 3 and 3 bis). Buses: 26, 96.*
An area often neglected by visitors, Belleville is a lively, multi-ethnic district that sprawls over the second highest hill (420ft/128m) in the city. Originally a working-class area, in the 1980s artists and musicians started moving in attracted by the cheaper rents and the traditional look of the *quartier*, which has escaped modernization to some extent. A succession of different ethnic populations have also lived in the area and today you can find a Chinatown here.

Rue de Belleville – This road and its side streets such as **rue de Rébeval**, with their cafes, restaurants, and food shops, are responsible for Belleville's growing reputation among dedicated foodies. Renowned *chanteuse* Édith Piaf was born at no. 72.

Rue du Borrégo – At **no. 53** you can see a fragment of the wall **Mur des Otages**, a sad memento of the turbulent time of the brief workers'

government, the **Commune**. In a courtyard near the church of Notre-Dame-des-Otages, it marks the spot where 52 hostages (priests, nuns, Paris civilian guards) from Grande-Roquette prison were shot by the **communards** in 1871.

Rue des Cascades – This quaint narrow road is a reminder that once this area was a country village. There is a magnificent view over Paris from the corner of the steps of **rue Fernand-Raynaud**. Two small buildings at **nos. 42** and **17** conceal parts of the underground aqueduct that carried springwater from Belleville to the city.

Belleville villas and passages – Explore the winding streets south of **rue de Belleville** to find picturesque villas. **Passage de la Duée** is one of the narrowest streets in Paris (3.28ft/1m). In rue de la Duée look out for **villa Georgina**. Nearby is **rue du Télégraphe**. It was in this road that inventor **Claude Chappe** (1763–1805) and his brothers conducted their first experiments on the telegraph in 1793.

CANAL SAINT-MARTIN★

M *République (lines 3, 5, 8, 9, and 11), Jaurès (lines 2, 5, and 7b).*
For a break from the crowds take a stroll along Canal Saint-Martin, a pretty watercourse straddled with iron footbridges and locks, and lined with trees. Completed in 1825, it connects with the Canal de l'Ourq at La Villette.

Tour – Along the canal

✕ **Lunch stop** – Quai de Valmy.

▷ *From République, take rue du Faubourg-du-Temple to blvd Jules-Ferry. Turn left onto square Frédéric-Lemaître.*

Square Frédéric-Lemaître – The canal disappears below ground to the south and resurfaces at the Port de Plaisance near the Seine *(see p 60)*. You can follow the canal to the north from here as it climbs through nine locks.

▷ *For a detour to Hôpital St-Louis, take ave Richerand to the right.*

St-Louis Hospital – Opened in 1618 to isolate plague victims from the rest of the city, this is one of the oldest Parisian hospitals. Its beautiful **central courtyard★** is reminiscent of the place des Vosges. Pioneering work in dermatology was carried out here.

▷ *Return to the canal.*

Square des Récollets – Take the **swing bridge** over the canal at **rue de la Grange** to find this small square separated by two footbridges. It is named after the former Franciscan Convent that stood nearby at 150 rue

des Récollets. On a darker note, the huge **Montfaucon Gallows** loomed over the area from the Middle Ages until 1760. The corpses were left to rot here for months. **Hôtel du Nord** *(102 quai de Jemmapes)* lent its name to the legendary film by Marcel Carné. Today it is a café-restaurant.

▷ *Continue along the canal to pl de la Bataille-de-Stalingrad.*

Rotonde de la Villette – *Place de la Bataille-de-Stalingrad.* Designed by Ledoux in the late 18C in the Neoclassical style, it was once a Parisian toll house and part of the old city wall, but is now used to store archeological finds.

▷ *Behind the Rotonde de la Villette, follow the left-hand quay of the Bassin de la Villette.*

This section of the waterway was built to connect the St-Martin and Ourcq canals. Finish by watching the impressive **transporter bridge** across the canal at rue de Crimée open to let boats through.

▷ *The Crimée Métro station is nearby, or follow the other side of the Bassin to the Jean-Jaurès Métro station.*

Strolling along the Canal Saint-Martin

© Y. Kanazawa / MICHELIN

RÉPUBLIQUE

Ⓜ *Temple (line 3), Réaumur-Sébastopol (lines 3 and 4), Arts-et-Métiers (lines 3 and 11), République (lines 3, 5, 8, 9, and 11).*

A popular area for an evening out, it is also rich in history. A fortress built by the Knights Templar was located here until they fell from grace in 1307, and the royal family were imprisoned in the Temple Tower on August 13, 1792.

Conservatoire national des Arts et Métiers★★ – This former Benedictine priory became a conservatoire for technical studies under the Convention in 1794. Today it also houses the **Musée des Arts et Métiers★★** *(01 53 01 82 00; www.arts-et-metiers.net; open Tue–Sun 10am–6pm, Thu 9.30pm; closed public holidays; 6.50€).* This fascinating museum highlights the worlds of science and industry, with displays ranging from an early flying machine to clocks and automata and an original Foucault pendulum. The 13C **monastery's refectory★★** can be seen in the courtyard on the right.

Église St-Nicolas-des-Champs★ – *254 rue St Martin. 01 42 72 92 54. www.asaintnicolas.com. See website for opening times.* This lovely 12C church with its Romanesque east end, fine capitals, belfry, and Gothic nave has been modified and enlarged over the centuries. Inside are fine paintings and an altarpiece by Simon Vouet.

Place de la République – This imposing square designed by Haussmann in 1854 was

Original Foucault pendulum, Musée des Arts et Métiers

© Christophe Lehenaff / Photononstop

completely reconfigured in 2013 to be more pedestrian-friendly. The ornate central monument commemorates the proclamation of the Third Republic in 1870. Created by Léonard and Charles Morice after they won a competition in 1879, it was inaugurated on 14 July 1883.

Square and Carreau du Temple – The Carreau du Temple *(4 rue Eugène Spuller. www.carreau dutemple.eu. Open Mon–Sat 1–7pm),* a 19th-century covered market converted into a multi-purpose arts and entertainment center in 2014, is on the site of a former fortress built by the Knights Templar, which later became the Temple Prison. The Temple acquired notoriety when the royal family were imprisoned there during the Revolution, and was eventually pulled down under the orders of Napoléon.

CIMETIÈRE DU PÈRE-LACHAISE★

Ⓜ *Père-Lachaise (lines 2 and 3). 01 55 25 82 10. www.pere-lachaise.com. Open mid-Mar–early Nov 8am–6pm, Sat 8.30am–6pm, Sun and public holidays 9am–6pm; early Nov–mid-Mar 8am–5.30pm, Sat 8.30am–5.30pm, Sun and public holidays 9am–5.30pm.*

Paris's largest cemetery is renowned not only for its size—it spreads over 99acres/40ha—and famous inhabitants—including Chopin, Edith Piaf, Balzac, Proust, Oscar Wilde, Colette, and Jim Morrison—but also for its romantic tombs and remarkable statuary. The cemetery is now a national heritage site and contains major monuments: **Le Mur des Fédérés** (Federalists' Wall) commemorates the last insurgents of the Paris **Commune** who are buried here in a communal grave, and nearby is a monument dedicated to the resistance movement and deportees of World War II. Also look out for the statue of Victor Noir, lying dramatically in a prone position. He was killed by a cousin of Napoléon III. George Rodendach seems to be rising from the grave with an outstretched arm.

To find your way around, pick up a map at Porte des Amandiers or Porte Gambetta.

Village de Charonne –
If you would like to explore the surrounding district, head for this small, tranquil village area not far from Père-Lachaise. The **Église St-Germain-de-Charonne★** *(place St-Blaise)* was the focal point of the village and dates from the 12C and 13C. This charming church has its own small cemetery. Rue St-Blaise leading off the square in front of the church used to be the main thoroughfare of the village and is now a pretty, partly pedestrianized street. Carefully restored 19C houses at **square des Grès★** and **rue Vitruve** mingle with more modern buildings.

La Campagne à Paris★ – A little farther on, close to the Porte de Bagnolet Métro station, "the country in Paris" is the name given to the 90 or so houses that were built for workers here on the site of a quarry that had been filled in with material from digging the Métro. Unusually for Paris, they have small front and rear gardens, contributing to the village feel.

Cimetière du Père-Lachaise

© S. Sauvignier / MICHELIN

LANDMARKS

As all major cities, Paris has its fair share of iconic monuments. The Eiffel Tower and the Arc de Triomphe simply "shout" Paris—you only have to see a picture of either to know instantly where you are.

ARC DE TRIOMPHE★★★

🚇 *Charles-de-Gaulle-Étoile (lines 1, 2, and 6). 01 55 37 73 77. www.arc-de-triomphe.monuments-nationaux.fr. Arch platform: Open Apr–Sept 10am–11pm; Oct–Mar 10am–10.30pm. Closed Jan 1, May 1 and 8 (morning), Jul 14 (morning), Nov 11 (morning), Dec 25. 9.50€.*

Monumental is a very apt description for this arch in **place Charles-de-Gaulle★★★**. Built to celebrate Napoléon's victories, it is a powerful modern icon too, and features in the celebrations on many national occasions, such as the 1989 bicentenary of the French Revolution. Commissioned by **Napoléon** in 1806, the arch is 164ft/50m high, 147.6ft/45m wide, and is decorated with magnificent sculpted reliefs.

Highlights:

♦ The **arch platform** From here is a superb **view★★★** of the city, halfway between the **Arc de Triomphe du Carrousel★** at the Louvre and the **Grande Arche★★** at La Défense.

♦ The **sculpted reliefs** The four groups at the base of the arch include *The Departure of the Volunteers* by Rude, more famously known as **La Marseillaise★★** since its depiction of the French withstanding their enemies aroused patriotic fervor.

♦ The **tomb of the Unknown Soldier** The Unknown Soldier was laid to rest here in 1921 beneath an eternal flame.

🏰 EIFFEL TOWER★★★

🚇 *Bir-Hakeim (line 6), École Militaire (line 8). 01 44 11 23 23. www.tour-eiffel.fr. Elevator: mid-Jun–end Aug 9am–12.45am (11pm for the top), early Sept–mid-Jun 9.30am–11.45pm (10:30pm for the top). 15€ (3rd floor). Stairs (1st and 2nd floor only): mid-Jun–end Aug 9am–12.45am, early Sept–mid-Jun 9.30am–6.30pm. 5€.*

When Gustave Eiffel completed the Tower in 1889 it became the tallest building in the world at 984ft/300m (TV aerials add another 68ft/20.75m). It contains 2.5 million rivets and weighs about 7,000 tons. In strong wind the maximum sway at the top is 4.7in/12cm. Depending on the temperature the height can vary by as much as 6in/15cm. There are three platforms for stunning views of Paris. From the third, the **view★★★** extends 42mi/67km in ideal conditions. The best time

Eiffel Tower

© Ilpo Musto / Apa Publications

Pont Alexandre III at dusk

© Paul Reid / Dreamstime.com

to see it is usually one hour before sunset when, on a clear day, the light is just right. Inside you will find restaurants, boutiques, and a museum.

LES INVALIDES★★★

Ⓜ *Invalides, Varenne, St-François-Xavier (all line 13). 01 44 42 38 77. www.invalides.org. Open Apr–Oct 10am–6pm; Nov–Mar 10am–5pm. Closed 1st Mon in month, Jan 1, May 1, Nov 1 (morning), Dec 25. 9.50€.*

Founded in 1670 by Louis XIV as a home for over 4,000 elderly and infirm soldiers, it still provides care for wounded veterans. The star attraction is **Napoléon's tomb**, but you can also learn about France's military history (see **Musée de l'Armée★★★**, *p84*).

Highlights:

◆ **Église du Dôme★★★**
A magnificent church completed in 1735, it is sumptuously decorated with low-relief sculptures and painted cupolas. The dome is ornamented with trophies, garlands, and a fine gold lantern. **Napoléon** is buried here in the kind of grand

tomb that befits an emperor, directly beneath the dome. The entrance to the crypt is guarded by two huge bronze statues.

◆ **L'Hôtel des Invalides★★★**
Designed according to ideal Classical proportions, the beautiful **façade★★** has twin pavilions flanking the imposing entrance on esplanade des Invalides. Just in front are formal gardens, lined with 17C and 18C cannons.

◆ **Musée des Plans reliefs★★**
A fascinating collection of scale models of towns and fortresses from the 17C to the present.

◆ **Pont Alexandre III★★** Built for the 1900 World Exhibition, this ornate bridge is a perfect example of *belle époque* style.

◆ **Cour d'honneur★** Napoléon would review his veterans here. Today you can see military artifacts and Napoléon's equestrian statue, which once stood on top of the column in **place Vendôme★★**.

◆ **Église de St-Louis-des-Invalides★** Also known as the soldiers' church, it contains a stunning 17C organ. Berlioz's *Requiem* debuted here in 1837.

73

🔔 CATHÉDRALE NOTRE-DAME★★★

🚇 *Cité, St Michel (both line 4).*
*01 42 34 56 10. www.cathedralede
paris.com. Open Mon–Fri 8am–
6.45pm, Sat–Sun 8am–7.15pm.
Guided tours in English Wed and
Thu 2pm, Sat 2.30pm.*

A breathtaking masterpiece of French art and architecture, Notre-Dame is the largest galleried church and one of the first to be supported by flying buttresses. Designed to rival the basilica in St Denis, near Paris, construction began in 1163 and even before it was completed major ceremonies were taking place here. The building suffered greatly during the Revolution, when a great deal of religious imagery was destroyed, but during the 19C it underwent major restoration masterminded by Viollet-le-Duc and Lassus.

Don't miss:

- The **West Front**, built to an asymmetrical medieval design. In the Middle Ages the statues would have stood against a gold background and been brightly colored.
- The **Portal of the Virgin** with its fine tympaneum.
- The **Portal of Saint Anne**, containing the oldest two statues of the cathedral.
- The **Portal of the Last Judgement**, restored by Viollet-le-Duc after it was heavily damaged by Revolutionaries in 1792.
- The **Rose window**, which is nearly 32.8ft/10m across, and the statue of the **Virgin and Child** in front of it.
- The **towers** rising to a height of 226.4ft/69m, which offer a marvelous **view★★★** of the spire, flying buttresses, and the city beyond.
- The **North Side** with its magnificent **Cloister Portal** that maximizes the light allowed into the interior.
- The **East End** and the fine views of **flying buttresses** and the 295ft/90m-high **spire** reconstructed by Viollet-le-Duc.
- The **South Side** and the superb sculpted doorway of St Stephen.
- The **interior** where the height (114.8ft/35m), length (426.5ft/130m), and width (157.4ft/48m) of the building alone are simply awe-inspiring.
- The **organ**, which contains more pipes than any other in the whole of France.
- The individual **chapels** of the guilds and noble families lining the sides of the cathedral between the buttresses.
- The **Treasury** in the Sacristy, built by Viollet-le-Duc, which holds precious relics, manuscripts, and ornaments, including the Crown of Thorns, the Holy Nail, and a fragment of the True Cross, and bishops' copes.

Place de la Concorde

© Didier Zylberyng / Pictures Colour Library

PLACE DE LA CONCORDE★★★

🅼 *Cité, St Michel (both line 4).*
This large, elegant square has seen bloody times in French history. During the Revolution a guillotine was erected in the north-west corner for the execution of **Louis XVI**. It was to claim another 1,343 victims, including Marie-Antoinette, before the square was renamed place de la Concorde in the late 1790s.

Highlights:

◆ The **views★★★** From the obelisk there are marvelous views up the Champs-Élysées toward the Arc de Triomphe and across the Tuileries toward the Louvre.

◆ **Obelisk★** Given to France by Mohammed Ali, Viceroy of Egypt, in 1831, the 3,300-year-old obelisk from the ruins of the temple at Luxor is made of pink granite. It is covered in hieroglyphics, weighs 220 tons, and stands 75.5ft/23m tall.

◆ **Pont de la Concorde** Completed in 1791, the bridge was made with stones from the Bastille prison. Built to replace the former ferry crossing at this point, it was widened in the 1930s and renovated in the 1980s.

SAINTE-CHAPELLE★★★

🅼 *Cité (line 4). 01 53 40 60 97. www.sainte-chapelle.monuments-nationaux.fr. Open Mar–Oct 9.30am–6pm; Nov–Feb 9.30am–5pm. Closed Jan 1, May 1, Dec 1 and 25. 8.50€.*
Representing a highpoint of Gothic architecture, the beautiful Holy Chapel is a masterpiece in stone and glass. It was commissioned

Sainte-Chapelle

©Katja Sucker / Fotolia.com

by St Louis (Louis IX) in the 13C to house holy relics and was consecrated in 1248. Consisting of two chambers, the upper was used by the sovereign and the lower by his household.

Don't miss:

◆ The stunning **upper chamber** is a wall-to-wall **stained glass** depiction of biblical stories, around 720 panes of which are original and the oldest in Paris.

◆ The **great windows** (49ft/15m high); there is so much glass in these that it is hard to spot the stonework between them.

◆ The **rose window** of the 15C depicting the Apocalypse.

◆ The **statues of the Apostles** attached to the pillars of the upper chamber. Six of them are original, although the painting is modern.

◆ The **spire** (108ft/33m high) is made from carved cedar wood. It is the fifth version to sit on top of the chapel and is a faithful replica of the original.

LANDMARKS

Opéra Garnier

© S. Sauvignier / MICHELIN

L'OPÉRA-GARNIER/ PARIS OPÉRA★★

Ⓜ *Opéra (lines 3, 7, and 8).
08 92 89 90 90. www.visitepalais-garnier.fr. Open daily 10am–5pm
(except during matinée or special
event). Guided tours of public
foyers and museum Wed, Sat, Sun
11.30am and 2.30pm (daily Jul–
Aug). Closed Jan 1 and May 1.
10€ (14€ with tour).*

The home of the Opéra National de
Paris, L'Opéra-Garnier has recently
been completely restored inside

The facts behind the fiction

The famous tale concocted by
Gaston Leroux has more
factual basis than you might think.
The marshy and unstable ground
upon which the Opéra was built
was indeed found to have a lake
beneath it, as described in the
novel. Fed by an underground
stream, it caused great problems
during construction as water
had to be pumped out before
the foundations could be laid.
And in 1896 there was a terrible
accident inside the building when
one of the counterweights of the
chandeliers fell and killed one of
the patrons.

---

and out. It was built during the
reign of Napoléon III by **Charles
Garnier**, at the time a 35-year-
old unknown architect. The very
grand and imposing main façade
is decorated with sculpted figures
and overlooks **place de l'Opéra★★**.
Inside★★★ the vast stage holds
up to 450 performers, but it is the
opulent use of multicolored French
marbles and the splendid **Great
Staircase** and **Grand Foyer** that
make attending a performance of
the opera or ballet a memorable
event. It is also the setting for the
Gothic novel by Gaston Leroux *The
Phantom of the Opera*.

LE PANTHÉON★★

Ⓜ *Luxembourg (line B). 01 44 32
18 00. www.pantheon.monuments-nationaux.fr. Open Apr–Sept
Tue–Sun 10am–6.30pm; Oct–Mar
Tue–Sun 10am–6pm. Guided tours
in French Apr–Oct. Closed public
holidays. 7.50€.*

Now the last resting place of the
great and the good of French
history, including Voltaire,
Rousseau, Victor Hugo, Émile Zola,
Louis Braille, and Pierre and Marie
Curie, Louis XV commissioned the
huge, solid Panthéon on recovering
from an illness in 1744. In 2002,

MUST SEE

Alexandre Dumas, author of *The Three Musketeers*, was reburied here, 132 years after his death.

Basilique du Sacré-Cœur

© S. Sauvignier / MICHELIN

What's outside?
♦ The **grand dome**★★.
♦ The **sculpted pediment** of Liberty handing crowns of laurel to the Nation.

What's inside?
♦ A fine **view**★★ over Paris from the Dome gallery.
♦ **Paintings**★ by 19C artists, including Delaunay, Maillot, and Puvis de Chavannes.
♦ **Frescoes** of scenes from the life of St Geneviève.
♦ The **crypt** holding the tombs of great French men and women.
♦ The site where **Léon Foucault** used a pendulum to prove the Earth rotates on an axis.

BASILIQUE DU SACRÉ-CŒUR★★

Ⓜ *Anvers (line 2). 01 53 41 89 00. www.sacre-coeur-montmartre.com. Dome: Open summer 8.30am–8pm; winter 9am–5pm. 6€. Crypt: Open daily 9am–5pm.*
Perched on Montmartre Hill (Butte Montmartre), the tall, white silhouette of the neo-Roman-Byzantine basilica is a distinctive feature of the Paris skyline, with its pointed cupolas and striking 262.4ft/80m-high campanile. It was built by public subscription following the disastrous Franco-Prussian War of 1870 after a group of Catholics vowed to erect a church to the Sacred Heart here. Building work began in 1876 and concluded in 1914. The church was consecrated in 1919 since when it has attracted countless pilgrims and visitors.

What's outside?
♦ A **panorama**★★★ extending for over 18.6mi/30km on a clear day from the external gallery of the dome.
♦ Another marvelous and much photographed **view**★★ over the capital from the church steps, especially at sunset.
♦ **Square Willette**, the garden in front of the basilica, which was laid out in 1929.
♦ A **funicular train**, which shuttles up the hill to the basilica and Montmartre and saves you a steep climb for the price of a Métro ticket.
♦ The **bronze doors** of the portico decorated with a sculpted relief of the Last Supper.
♦ The bell **La Savoyarde** in the campanile, which is one of the heaviest bells in the world (19t). Cast in 1895 at Annecy, it was a gift from the dioceses of Savoy.

What's inside?
♦ **Brightly colored mosaics** by Luc Olivier Merson.
♦ Climb the spiral staircase to the **dome** for a great view of the interior of the basilica.
♦ The **crypt** containing relics and treasures, and there is also an audiovisual display on the history and cult of the basilica too.

LANDMARKS

77

NEW PARIS

You could not accuse the planners and architects of Paris of being afraid of the new. Delighting in innovation, they juxtapose contemporary design against the classic lines of traditional Parisian elegance.

LA DÉFENSE★★

Ⓜ *Esplanade de la Défense (line 1),* Ⓜ*/RER: Grande Arche de la Défense (line 1/A). Buses: 73, 141, 144, 161, 174, 178, 258, 262, 272.*

With its ultra modern mix of ambitious experimental architecture, art, and gleaming skyscrapers, the business district of La Défense is full of examples of contemporary architecture and design. Located at the far west of the axis that starts at the Louvre and passes through the Arc de Triomphe, the Grande Arche dominates this mini Manhattan.

Tour of the architectural highlights ★★

✕ **Lunch stop** – rue de Bezons.

▷ *Start the walk in place Carpeaux.*

La Grande Arche – *Esplanade de la Défense.* Designed by Otto von Specklensen, this enormous arch is so tall (361ft/110m) that Notre-Dame could fit inside it. The views over Paris are impressive, although the rooftop platform is no longer open to the public.

La Grande Arche

© Michal Bednarek / Dreamstime.com

Built in 1958, the **Palais de la Défense (CNIT)**★ convention center, is notable for its large unsupported concrete span.

▷ *In place de la Défense.*

Inventor of the mobile **Alexander Calder**'s last work, a red stabile sculpture 49ft/15m high.

▷ *Turn left and walk through the opening to the Fiat Tower.*

Reminiscent of the monolith in *2001: A Space Odyssey*, the entirely black **Tour Areva** (previously Framatone), close to the **Elf Tower**, is the tallest building at 584ft/178m high.

▷ *Return to the esplanade de la Défense and the* ***monumental fountain*** *by Agam.*

The **Moretti Tower** is covered in 672 colored tubes. **Tour Manhattan** is a huge skyscraper full of offices, unusual for being curved in shape rather than rectangular.

▷ *Turn left in front of the* ***Tour Gan,*** *shaped like a Greek cross.*

Les Miroirs fountain by Henri La Fonta is made of ten mosaic-decorated cylinders.

▷ *Return to the esplanade de la Défense.*

MUST SEE

At the east end of the esplanade, the **Bassin de Takis** is a pool of water into which have been mounted 49 metal poles bearing multicolored lights. They make a great display at night when they flash and sway on top of the poles. **Tour Hoechst-Marion-Roussel** was the first high-rise to be built in the district in 1967.

◯ *Turn back toward La Grande Arche.*

A futuristic, brightly colored **sculpture by Miro** of two figures stands before the Quatre Temps shopping complex.

THE PYRAMID★★ AT THE LOUVRE

Ⓜ *Palais-Royal – Musée du Louvre (lines 1 and 7).*
When this glass pyramid, 69ft/21m high and 108ft/33m wide at its base, was opened as the new main entrance to the **Louvre★★★** *(see Landmarks)* in 1989 it caused some controversy. Designed by **Ieoh Ming Pei** and built of glass supported in stainless steel tubes, it is surrounded by three smaller pyramids. For an unusual view of the main pyramid, head downstairs to the reception area of the Louvre, which lies directly below it.

LA VILLETTE★★

Ⓜ *Porte de la Villette (North: Cité des Sciences et de l'Industrie, line 7) and Porte de Pantin (South: Cité de la Musique, line 5). Buses: 75, 139, 150, 152.*
Opened in 1986 and built on the site of the huge city slaughterhouses, La Villette was designed by architect Adrien Fainsilber and is home to the city's largest park. It offers plenty of green space in which to relax and lots of things to keep children amused, with a modern museum and entertainment complex set amid ten themed gardens. Dotted about the complex are a number of modern follies, some of which have now been converted into cafés.

Cité des Sciences et de l'Industrie★★★

30 avenue Corentin-Cariou. 01 40 05 80 00. www.cite-sciences.fr. See map p 80.
Combining light, water, and greenery, this interactive science and technology complex in a contemporary setting has achieved great success. It manages to inform, teach, and entertain all at the same time. It houses the **Explora★★** and the **Cité des Enfants**.

The Louvre and the Pyramid

© S. Sauvignier / MICHELIN

NEW PARIS

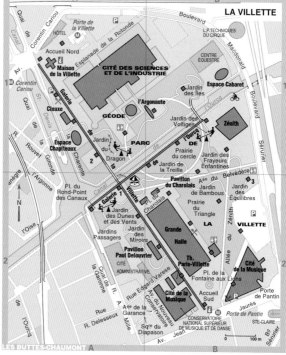

Médiathèque – *Levels 1 and 2 for adults; ground floor for children.* As well as books and other printed material, there is a wide range of multimedia available.

L'Argonaute, Cité des Enfants, Explora★★, La Géode★★, *see For Kids*
Cité de la Musique *see Live Music and Dance*

BERCY★

Ⓜ *Bercy (lines 6 and 14), Cour St Émilion (line 14). Buses: 24, 87.*
In the 1990s this site, which had been occupied by warehouses and industrial buildings belonging to

the wine trade, was transformed into an entertainment district. Stores and cinemas were built and a riverside park was created, and Bercy's large stadium (the **Palais Omnisports**) was erected, which hosts major sporting events and concerts *(see Sports and Activities)*. The exterior walls of the stadium slope at an angle of 45 degrees and are covered in grass.
The Ministry of Finance relocated here, too, in an imposing contemporary structure. The **Cinémathèque française** is housed in the former American Center, designed by Frank Ghery. *(See Stage and Screen).*

Bibliothèque Nationale de France: site François-Mitterand★

01 53 79 59 59. www.bnf.fr. Open Tue–Sat 9am–7pm, Mon 2–7pm, Sun 1–7pm. Closed public holidays and 3 weeks in Sept. 3.50–9€.
Dominique Perrault built this contemporary complex of buildings in the shape of four open books (appropriately enough) to house the national collection. The library, to which most of the national collection was transferred in 1998, stands on a vast rectangular esplanade lined with trees.

Cour St-Émilion – Bercy village★

A pedestrian-only street with boutiques, cafés, restaurants and cinema housed in the renovated stone warehouses of the former wine district.

Parc de Bercy "memory gardens"★

There are three gardens to enjoy here: one of extensive grass lawns, a romantic garden with water features and a labyrinth, and last, a more hardworking area with an orchard, a vegetable garden, a vineyard, and a rose garden.

The Ministry of Finance

Commissioned by François-Mitterrand, the new building housing the ministry dominates the area. The government department moved here from its original premises in the Louvre.

INSTITUT DU MONDE ARABE★

Ⓜ *Jussieu. 1 rue des Fossés-Saint-Bernard. 01 40 51 38 38.*

Window of Institute du Monde arabe

www.imarabe.org. Open Tue–Sun 10am–6pm (Fri until 9.30pm, Sat–Sun until 7pm). Closed May 1. No charge for entry to building. Museum 8€.
The institute was founded by France and 20 Arab countries to promote Islamic culture, cultural exchanges, and cooperation. A wide range of art and decorative objects from the 9C to the present day is on display in the **museum and exhibition spaces**. There are also exhibits of Islamic discoveries in the fields of mathematics, medicine, and astronomy, including a collection of astrolabes with which the stars could be observed and their positions calculated before the invention of the sextant.
The building was designed by Jean Nouvel. The outer structure is built of glass and aluminum and is covered with a sheath of translucent alabaster.

Windows on the world

The windows of the Institut du Monde arabe consist of light-sensitive screens that open and close in response to the conditions outside, enabling the amount of light entering the building to be controlled.

MAJOR MUSEUMS

The streets of Paris may be full of history, art, and architecture, but its outstanding museums are rich with unique collections that will enable you to explore deeper whatever your interest, from Egyptian antiquities and the military to art and fashion.

LE GRAND LOUVRE★★★

Ⓜ *Palais-Royal–Musée du Louvre (lines 1 and 7). 01 40 20 53 17. www.louvre.fr. Open Wed–Mon 9am–6pm (Wed and Fri some sections until 9.45pm). Closed Jan 1, May 1, Nov 11, Dec 25. 12€.*

You can't help but find the Louvre awe-inspiring. It is one of the greatest collections of art and antiquities in the world with over 350,000 exhibits cataloged, including many that have been reproduced in books and magazines hundreds of times. Since the first fortress was built here in 1190 it has been the seat of many rulers, each of whom modified and expanded the building over the centuries to create the magnificent palace we see today. They also acquired many of the Louvre's superb works. By the time Louis XIV died, in 1715, there were over 2,500 paintings in the palaces of the Louvre and Versailles.

Cour Carrée

© Daniel Thierry / Photononstop / Tips Images

What's outside?

◆ **Cour Carrée★★★** At night this elegant Renaissance façade is lit up to atmospheric effect.

◆ **Colonnade★★** Classical grandeur and harmony, commissioned by Louis XIV in 1662.

◆ **Pyramid★★** *see New Paris*

◆ **Arc de Triomphe du Carrousel★** The eastern-most arch of the **historic vista★★★** from the Louvre to the Grande Arche at La Défense, this monument was built 1806–8, and celebrates Napoléon's victory at the Battle of Austerlitz in 1805.

What's inside?

◆ **Medieval Louvre★★★** Discover the early history of the palace in a self-guided tour.

◆ **History of the Louvre★** Two galleries present the story of the palace since the 13C.

◆ **Carrousel du Louvre** A large underground shopping complex. *(See Shopping)*

The Collection

Deciding which galleries to visit can be a problem, given the sheer scale of what's on offer—here are some ideas.

Highlights:

◆ **Egyptian Antiquities★★★** (Sully, ground floor) An exceptional collection, it includes the **Seated Scribe★★★**

and one of the earliest known knives, **Knife of Gebel-el-Arak★★**.

♦ **Greek Antiquities★★★** (Denon, ground floor) One of the many jewels in the Louvre, featuring the serene **Venus de Milo★★★** and the **Winged Victory of Samothrace★★★** (on a pedestal above Escalier Daru). **Salle des Caryatides★★**, now a Greek gallery, was the great hall of the old Louvre palace.

♦ **Near-Eastern Antiquities★★★** (Richelieu, ground floor) The collection includes outstanding **reliefs★★** from Ashurbanipal palace at Nineveh.

♦ **Etruscan Antiquities★★** (Richelieu, ground floor) Don't miss the **Sarcophagus of the Married Couple★★★**. Dating from 6C BC, it is a charming portrait of a devoted couple.

♦ **Islamic art★★** Opened in 2012, this new gallery displays 3000 objects from the Islamic world.

♦ **French painting★★★** (Denon, first floor and Sully, second floor) The extensive collection is rich in masterpieces, including Théodore Géricault's **The Raft of the Medusa★★** and Eugène Delacroix's **Liberty Leading the People★★**.

♦ **Italian painting★★★** (Denon, second floor) One of the glories of the Louvre. When you are finally standing in front of the **Mona Lisa★★★**, the most famous painting in the world, it is an almost surreal moment. Nearby is Veronese's **Wedding at Cana★★★**. You can also see works by Raphael and Caravaggio's **The Fortune Teller★★**.

♦ **Northern European painting ★★★** (Richelieu, second floor) Be sure to see the **Madonna with Chancellor Rolin★★** by Jan van Eyck, **The Moneylender and his Wife★★** by Quentin Metsys, as well as the beautiful works by **Rubens** and **Vermeer van Delft**.

♦ **Spanish painting★★** (Denon, second floor) El Greco's **Christ on the Cross★★** typifies Spanish paintings' rich mix of realism and mysticism.

♦ **Sculpture galleries★★★** (Denon and Richelieu, ground floor) Among the finest works are **Slaves★★★** by **Michelangelo** and Canova's **Psyche Revived by the Kiss of Cupid★★**.

♦ **Objets d'Art★★** (Richelieu, first floor) A superb collection featuring the **medieval treasure of the Louvre★★★**.

♦ **Napoléon III Apartments★★★** (Richelieu, first floor, gallery 87) A rare example of Second Empire decor, which has survived intact with the original furnishings—an opulent world of crimson and gold.

MAJOR MUSEUMS

MUSÉE DE L'ARMÉE★★★

L'Hôtel des Invalides. 01 44 42 38 77. www.invalides.org. Open Apr–Sept 10am–6pm (last admission 30 min before closing); Oct–Mar 10am–5pm. Closed 1st Mon in the month, Jan 1, May 1, Nov 1, Dec 25. 9.50€ (includes entry to the Eglise du Dôme - Napoléon's Tomb).
If you're interested in the military you're in for a treat with one of the world's richest army museums. It contains over 500,000 exhibits, covering weapons and armor from prehistoric times to the present day.

Highlights:

♦ The story of the **evolution of war**.
♦ **Weapons** and **suits of armor** from earliest times to the 19C.
♦ Souvenirs and weapons relating to **Napoléon's campaigns**.
♦ **Artillery** from across the centuries.
♦ **Military banners**.
♦ Maps telling the story of the battlefields of **World War I**.
♦ A major **World War II** display, vividly told through video, personal objects, and images,

dating from the French army's defeat in 1940 via the Free French Forces and the Resistance movement to the capitulation of Japan.

If you're keen to see some more military hardware, head for the **Cour d'honneur★** where there is an impressive display of cannons: two to look out for are the *Catherina* (1487) and the highly decorated *Württemberg* culverin (16C). More modern pieces include a Renault tank and a Marne taxi, which was used to carry soldiers to the front in World War I.

MUSÉE NATIONAL DES ARTS ASIATIQUES – GUIMET★★★

Ⓜ *Iéna (line 9). 6 pl d'Iéna. 01 56 52 53 00. www.guimet.fr. Open Tue–Sun 10am–6pm (Dec 24 and 31 5pm). Closed Jan 1, May 1, Dec 25. 7.50€.*
Step into the Musée Guimet, and enter a totally different world. This superb collection of Oriental art was founded by Émile Guimet, a 19C industrialist who traveled throughout Asia. Ranging from a colossal statue of Nâga, a seven-headed stone serpent from Cambodia, to delicate Chinese **Ming porcelain★**, you'll find a great variety of exhibits. Among the many highlights is an area dedicated to **Khmer (Cambodian) art★★**, and Japanese decorative and fine art, including Hokusai's **Wave off the coast of Kanagawa★★**. There is also a unique collection of Buddhist art in the **Galeries du panthéon bouddhique de la Chine et du Japon** (*Hôtel Heidelbach, 19 avenue d'Iéna; opening times as above*).

Musée Guimet

Musée des Arts décoratifs

Batenciaga Paris

© Ilpo Musto / APA Publications

MUSÉE DES ARTS DÉCORATIFS★★

Ⓜ *Palais-Royal–Musée du Louvre (lines 1 and 7). 111 rue de Rivoli. www.lesartsdecoratifs.fr. Open Tue–Sun 11am–6pm. Closed Jan 1, May 1, Aug 15, Dec 25. 11€ (includes entry to Musée de la Mode et du Textile).*

Style and design are synonymous with France. To see how it developed visit this beautifully refurbished museum, with sculpture, painting, ceramics, furniture, jewelry, glass, and tableware from the Middle Ages to the 20C. The period room sets are particularly evocative. If fashion is your thing, then make the **Musée de la Mode et du Textile★** *(107 rue de Rivoli, see p 47)* your next stop. Featuring the outfits of Poiret, Lanvin, Schiaperelli, Dior, and Paco Rabanne among many others, the museum has a splendid collection of fashion and textiles since the 18C.

MUSÉE CARNAVALET – HISTOIRE DE PARIS★★

Ⓜ *Saint-Paul (line 1). Hôtel Carnavalet, 23 rue de Sévigné. 01 44 59 58 58. www.carnavalet. paris.fr. Open Tue–Sun 10am–6pm. Closed some public holidays. No charge for the permanent collection.*

For a lively overview of Parisian history, from Neolithic times via the Middle Ages, the French Revolution, and the Second Empire, the Musée Carnavalet is a great stop-off in the old Marais district. It is housed in two historic mansions, joined by a gallery—the Hôtel Carnavalet, where Madame Sévigné lived and wrote her famous letters to her daughter, and the Hôtel Le-Peletier-St-Fargeau. The many displays and reconstructions range from wooden Neolithic canoes found in Bercy in 1999 to reconstructions of the richly decorated drawing rooms from the Hôtel de la Rivière,

A writer's bedroom

In addition to his writing, such as his masterpiece *À la recherche du temps perdu (Rembrance of Things Past)*, Marcel Proust (1871–1922) is famous for the time he spent in his bed at 102 boulevard Haussmann. Chronically asthmatic and distracted by noise rising from the boulevard below, he preferred to work at night and sleep during the day. He even had the room lined with cork tiles and the windows covered with heavy curtains, which you can see in the Musée Carnavalet's authentic display made with his own furniture.

MAJOR MUSEUMS

painted by Lebrun, and the *belle époque* decor of the Fouquet jewelry shop. There are also many portraits, pieces of furniture, and souvenirs of the city's famous writers, in particular a replica of Marcel Proust's bedroom.

MUSÉE COGNACQ-JAY★★

🅜 *Saint-Paul (line 1). Hôtel Donon, 8 rue Elzévir. 01 40 27 07 21. www.cognacq-jay.paris.fr. Open Tue–Sun 10am–6 pm. Closed public holidays. No charge.*

Step back in time in the enchanting Musée Cognacq-Jay, which houses the 19C collection of Ernest Cognacq and Louise Jay, the founders of the Samaritaine department store. Together they created a treasure trove of fine and decorative European art and furniture from the finest 19C artists, beautifully displayed in a 16C town house in the Marais.

MUSÉUM NATIONAL D'HISTOIRE NATURELLE★★

Paris is not just about outstanding art, architecture, and style, it is also home to one of the world's greatest conservatories of natural science. Originally founded as the Royal Botanic Gardens in the 17C, it became the National Museum for Natural History during the Revolution in 1793. In the same year a menagerie was created here too, enabling Parisians to see animals such as elephants, bears, and giraffes for the first time.

Grande Galerie de l'Évolution★★★

🅜 *Gare D'Austerlitz (lines 5 and 10/C). 36 rue Geoffroy-Saint-Hilaire. 01 40 79 54 79. www.mnhn.fr. Open Wed–Mon 10am–6pm. Closed May 1. 7€.*

There are three fascinating areas to explore here: **the diversity of living species** (including a children's discovery room), the impact of human activity (level 2 in the **Galerie des Espèces menacées ou disparues★★**— endangered species), and the **history of evolutionary studies**. The museum's oldest stuffed animal can be found here too! It's a rhinoceros from Asia that belonged to Louis XV and Louis XVI.

Galerie de Minéralogie et de Géologie★

Open Apr–Oct Wed–Mon 10am–5pm. Closed May 1. Closed for renovations until late 2014.

See fabulous rare and **precious stones**, and **giant crystals, meteorites, and minerals**. There are also objets d'art and jewels from the collection of the Sun King Louis XIV.

Galeries de Paléontologie et d'Anatomie comparée

Open Apr–Oct Wed–Mon 10am–5pm. Closed May 1. 7€.

The museum holds an astounding 36,000 vertebrate specimens, but not all on display a same time, needless to say. The vast array of **fossils** is on the first and second floors, among reproductions of large prehistoric animals and extinct species.

Queen of Sheba, Musée National du Moyen Age

MUSÉE NATIONAL DU MOYEN ÂGE★★ – THERMES ET HÔTEL DE CLUNY

Ⓜ *Cluny-La Sorbonne (line 10). 6 pl Paul-Painlevé. 01 53 73 78 00. www.musee-moyenage.fr. Open Wed–Mon 9.15am–5.45pm (last admission 30min before closing). Closed Jan 1, May 1, Dec 25. 8.50€, no charge 1st Sun in the month.*
A fascinating museum set in the beautiful 15C Parisian residence of the abbots of Cluny, in the busy Left Bank area. This exquisite collection of medieval arts and treasures is alongside the ruins of a Roman baths.

Museum★★

Tucked away in this small museum are some of the finest masterpieces of the Middle Ages, including illuminated manuscripts, sculpture, and church furnishings. Not to be missed is the beautiful **La Dame à la Licorne**★★★ *(The Lady and the Unicorn, Room 13, 1st floor),* a superb example of 15C and early 16C Netherlandish tapestry representing allegories of the five senses and spiritual devotion.

Les Thermes★

The **Gallo-Roman public baths** are thought to date from AD 200. Although mostly destroyed in the 3C, the huge vaulted frigidarium (a cold-water bath) still stands.

Hôtel de Cluny

The building housing the museum is a 15C private Parisian house. It has been restored over the centuries, yet many medieval details survive, including the mullioned windows, a frieze, the flamboyant balustrade, and the gargoyles on the roof. The small **Chapel**★ on the first floor was designed as the abbot's oratory.

GRAND PALAIS★

Ⓜ *Concorde (lines 1, 8, and 12), Champs-Élysées-Clemenceau (lines 1 and 13). 3 ave du Général-Eisenhower. 01 44 13 17 17. www.grandpalais.fr. Open Wed–Sun 10am–8pm (Wed 10pm). Closed May 1 and Dec 25. 10€.*
This grand hall, built around 1900, hosts exhibitions from around the world. Check out what is on during your stay.

MUSÉE DU PETIT PALAIS★

Ⓜ *Concorde (lines 1, 8, and 12), Champs-Élysées-Clemenceau (lines 1 and 13). Ave Winston-Churchill. 01 53 43 40 00. www.petitpalais. paris.fr. Open Tue–Sun 10am–6pm. Closed public holidays. No charge for the permanent collection.*
This gem of a museum features a range of fine and decorative art from medieval times to the 19C. Look out for the *Good Samaritan* (1880) by **Aimé Morot** and *Ascension* (1879) by **Gustave Doré**.

MAJOR MUSEUMS

GREAT GALLERIES

You would expect to find some of the world's best galleries in Paris and the city doesn't disappoint. There is something for everyone, from unpredictable modern art in the Beaubourg via the vast space of the amazing Musée d'Orsay, to the Impressionist masterpieces in the Musée Marmottan-Monet.

MUSÉE NATIONAL D'ART MODERNE★★★

Ⓜ *Rambuteau (line 11). Pl Georges-Pompidou. 01 44 78 12 33. www.centrepompidou.fr. Open Wed–Sun 11am–9pm. Atelier Brancusi: 2–6pm. Closed May 1. Museum and exhibitions 13€, no charge for museum 1st Sun in month.*

For a taste of the modern and contemporary in art and architecture head for the Centre Georges-Pompidou and the Musée national d'Art moderne on the fourth and fifth levels. With 50,000 works and objects from 1905 to the present day, the gallery is one of the most important collections of 20C art in the world.

The modern collection (1905–60), starting with **Fauvism** and **Cubism**, is on the fifth floor. Galleries dedicated to single artists alternate with thematic rooms. Contemporary art from the 1960s onward is on the fourth floor with

works by Warhol among others. The Parisian sculpture workshop of **Constantin Brancusi** (1876–1957) has been reconstructed in its entirety in place Georges-Pompidou. You can see the studio in which the sculptor worked, complete with his tools and personal art collection.

Highlights modern collection:

♦ All the major movements, from **Fauvism** to the **Cobra** movement and **American art** of the 1940s to 1960s.

♦ Major works by **great masters**, including Matisse, Braque, Picassso, Modigliani, Duchamp, Chagall, Salvador Dali, Magritte, Pollock, Rothko, and Newman.

♦ Changing displays in the 40 galleries highlight major themes and artists to present an overview of the creative art scene during the first half of the 20C.

Musée national d'Art moderne, Centre Georges-Pompidou

© S. Sauvignier / MICHELIN

MUST SEE

Highlights contemporary collection:

- Changing displays feature the major names and artistic trends of the later 20C, including **Pop Art**, **New Realism**, and **Op** and **Kinetic Art**.
- Three galleries featuring design and architecture from the 1960s to the present day by figures such as Starck, Nouvel, Perrault, and Toto Ito.
- Displays focusing on the cinema, multimedia installations, and Happenings of the **Gutaï** and **Fluxus** groups.

If you need a breather after your journey through art, pop up to the sixth floor for a splendid **view★★** across the Paris rooftops. It can be accessed via the escalators in the transparent tube that climbs up the outside of the building (access to the view without museum entrance, 3€).

MUSÉE D'ORSAY★★★

Ⓜ️ *Solférino (line 12). 62 rue de Lille. 01 40 49 48 14. www.musee-orsay.fr. Open Tue–Sun 9.30am–6pm (Thu 9.45pm). Closed Jan 1, May 1, Dec 25. Permanent collection 11€, no charge 1st Sun in the month.*
A visit to Paris would not be complete without a trip to the Musée d'Orsay. Since its opening in 1986, the former Gare d'Orsay has served as a stunning showcase for the fine and decorative arts from 1848 to 1914. Its splendid setting overlooking the river matches the quality of the works in its collection.

Your visit

The collection is divided into major categories, including painting,

---

From station to museum

Turning a former railway station into an art gallery may seem a little strange, but thanks to the space and light of the former Gare d'Orsay the project has been very successful. Originally the terminal for the Paris–Orléans line, the go-ahead for its conversion was given in 1977. Before that it had also served as a reception center for prisoners on the Liberation of Paris and a set for a number of films.

---

sculpture, architecture, decorative arts, and photography. Before you enter the galleries, pick up a free plan of the museum at the reception desk. It will give you the latest information about where major works are displayed and will help you plan your route. In each room you can also refer to theme cards, or you can rent an audio guide. And, when your attention is finally wandering or your feet are tired, take a break in the café located behind one of the huge clocks.

Painting and Sculpture – The decades covered by the collection were extremely fruitful in terms of painting and sculpture.

Highlights include:

- **Neoclassicism and Romanticism** Works by sculptors and painters, including Cavelier, Pradier, Préault, Ingres, Chassériau, and Delacroix.
- **Realism** A glimpse of everyday life in the innovative work of Rosa Bonheur, Antigna, Fantin-Latour, Daumier, Millet (the

Musée d'Orsay seen across the Seine

© Camille Moirenc / Photononstop / Tips Images

Gleaners, 1857), and Courbet (*A Burial at Ornans*, 1849–50).

◆ **The Barbizon School** Rediscover the countryside through the eyes of Corot and Rousseau.

◆ **Academism** How French academic art developed through the work of the sculptors Fremiet, Carrier-Belleuse, and Carpeaux, and

the painters Cabanel, Gérôme, and Franz Winterhalter.

◆ **Symbolism** Interior worlds skillfully evoked by Camille Claudel and Rodin, Burne-Jones, Doré, Munch, Klimt, Puvis de Chavannes, and Moreau among many others.

◆ **Impressionists** All the greats are represented here, from the early days to the mature period. Renoir's *Dancing at Le Moulin de la Galette* (1876), Manet's *Dejeuner sur l'herbe* (1863) and *Olympia* (1863), Degas's *Little 14-Year-Old Dancer* (1881), Cézanne's *Bathers* (c 1890) and *The Cardplayers* (1890–95), Caillebotte's *Planing the Floor* (1875), and Monet's *Wind Effect, Series of The Poplars* (1891).

◆ **The Pont-Aven School** and **the Nabis** Gauguin's *Self-portrait with the Yellow Christ* (1889) and Bernard's *Breton Women with Umbrellas* (1892).

◆ **Neo-Impressionism** Complete your tour of the paintings with the bold visions of Matisse, Renoir, Cross, Signac, Cézanne, Seurat, Toulouse-Lautrec (*Jane Avril Dancing*, c 1892), and Van

---

Touring Tip

Make the most of your visit

Expect queues to buy an entry ticket, or buy it in advance through the website or at branches of the FNAC department store. A **Museum Pass** covers entrance on the same day to the permanent exhibitions at the Musée d'Orsay and Musée Rodin. A **Paris Museum Pass** can also be bought online (http://en.parismuseumpass.com) or at one of the venues. It gives free admission (no waiting in line) to more than 60 museums and monuments in Paris for 2, 4, or 6 days.

Gogh (*Dr Paul Gachet*, 1890, and *Bedroom in Arles*, 1889).

Architecture 1852–70 – The period covered is relatively limited, but don't miss the fascinating cross-section scale model of the Opéra-Garnier. It shows the stage and its machinery, but also the maze of passages and tunnels beneath the building.

Decorative and Applied Arts – How good design was combined with developing industrial processes during the period 1850–80 and the **Art Nouveau** period. Artists featured include Lalique, Van de Velde, Horta, Frank Lloyd Wright, and Charles Rennie Mackintosh.

Photography – Its evolution from 1839 to 1920. When it was decided to include photography in the museum, the collection had to be built up from scratch.

It contains 50,000 images of every type—slides, negatives, albums—by Stieglitz, Nadar, and Le Gray, among others.

MUSÉE MARMOTTAN-MONET★★

Ⓜ *La Muette (line 9). 2 rue Louis-Boilly. 01 44 96 50 33. www.marmottan.com. Open Tue–Sun 10am–6pm (Thu 8pm). Closed Jan 1, May 1, Dec 25. 10€.*
Not far from the Bois de Boulogne, this was the former home of the art historian Paul Marmottan, who built up his own collection here, bequeathing it with the house as a museum. Michel Monet left 65 of his father's paintings, plus notebooks and sketches, to the museum in 1971. Together with other paintings by Monet donated separately they represent the most important known collection of the artist's works and include *Impression – Sunrise*, which gave the **Impressionist** movement its name, *The Houses of Parliament –*

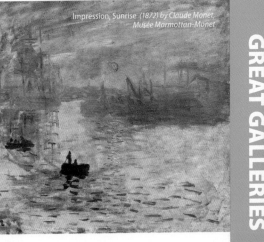

Impression, Sunrise *(1872) by Claude Monet, Musée Marmottan-Monet*

GREAT GALLERIES

Nymphéas by Claude Monet Musée de l'Orangerie

London, *The Europe Bridge*, *Rouen Cathedral*, and many paintings from Giverny, which absorbed Monet for the last 30 years of his life, depicting his beloved water lilies, wisteria, iris, rose-garden, weeping willows, and the pretty Japanese bridge. The Monet collection is wonderful but don't neglect the rest of the gallery. There are also rooms presenting works by many of his contemporaries, such as Manet, Morisot, and Degas, including Gauguin's splendid *Bouquet of Flowers* painted in Tahiti and Renoir's pastel *Seated Girl in a White Hat*.

MUSÉE DE L'ORANGERIE★★

Ⓜ *Concorde (lines 1, 8, and 12). Jardin des Tuileries. 01 44 77 80 07. www.musee-orangerie.fr. Open Wed–Mon 9am–6pm. Closed May 1, Dec 25. 9€, no charge 1st Sun of the month.*

Claude Monet's exquiste water lily series **Nymphéas★★★** is here, painted in his garden at Giverny. It is displayed to great effect around the walls of two oval rooms on the ground floor, built especially for the paintings. In the lower-level galleries you will find the **Walter-Guillaume Collection**. Founded by art dealer and collector Paul Guillaume, it presents the work

of many artists, including Soutine, Picasso, Modigliani, Cézanne, Renoir, Matisse, and Rousseau.

MUSÉE PICASSO★★

Ⓜ *Chemin Vert (line 8). Hôtel Salé, 5 rue de Thorigny. 01 42 71 25 21. www.musee-picasso.fr. Closed for refurbishment until summer 2014.*

Picasso enthusiasts usually head straight for Hôtel Salé, completely renovated and expanded between 2009–2014, with 4000 drawings, 300 paintings and 300 sculptures, as well as notebooks, collages, and engravings. Donated by Picasso's heirs following his death in 1973, it features works spanning his lifetime, including the *Self Portrait* from the Blue Period, *Still Life with Cane Chair* and *Pipes of Pan*, as well as female nudes, traveling acrobats, and portraits of his family.

MUSÉE RODIN★★

Ⓜ *Varenne or Invalides (both line 13). 77 rue de Varenne. 01 44 18 61 10. www.musee-rodin.fr. Open Tue–Sun 10am–5.45pm (Wed until 8.45pm). Closed Jan 1, May 1, Dec 25. 9€ (2€ for garden only), no charge 1st Sun of the month (last admission 5.15pm).*

Rodin's final home and studio in Paris is the perfect serene setting in which to enjoy his work. Once a

MUST SEE

magnificent mansion completed in 1730, Hôtel Biron had fallen on hard times when Rodin moved into a suite of rooms overlooking the garden in 1908. Other rooms were let to other artists such as Isadora Duncan, Jean Cocteau, Rainer Maria Rilke, and Matisse.

What's inside?

♦ Highlights of the museum's vast collection of 6,600 sculptures by Rodin, displayed in chronological order.

♦ Rodin's expressive sketches and paintings for his works.

♦ Plaster maquettes for large group pieces and for the final statues of Balzac and Victor Hugo, which can be seen in the museum garden.

♦ Works acquired by Rodin, such as *Le Père Tanguy* by Van Gogh and *Female Nude* by Renoir.

♦ Works by fellow sculptor and contemporary Camille Claudel, who was at one time Rodin's pupil, muse, and mistress.

What's outside?

♦ Some of Rodin's most famous sculptures: *The Thinker, The Burghers of Calais, The Gates*

of Hell, and *Ugolino and his Children*.

♦ Sculpture collected by Rodin, including the Roman *Headless Hercules*.

♦ A newly restored chapel featuring temporary exhibitions.

GALERIE NATIONALE DU JEU DE PAUME

Ⓜ *Concorde (lines 1, 8, and 12). 1 pl de Concorde. 01 47 03 12 50. www.jeudepaume.org. Open Tue–Fri 11am–7pm (Tue 9pm), Sat–Sun 10am–7pm. Free guided tour Tue–Sat 12.30pm. Closed Jan 1, May 1, Dec 25. 8.50€.*

For a change from painting and sculpture, make your way to Galerie nationale du Jeu de Paume. You will no longer find any tennis courts here—the building was erected in 1861 for this purpose. The associations of the Patrimoine Photographique and the Centre national de la Photographie have joined forces with the Jeu de Paume to create this contemporary art collection, comprising photography, film, and installations. It used to house the Impressionist Collection but this is now in the Musée d'Orsay (see p 89).

Photo: Adrien Chevrot © Jeu de Paume 2014

Jeu de Paume

PARKS AND GARDENS

At first sight Paris may not seem a particularly green city, but there are numerous green spaces—often in unexpected places—and parks and gardens are dotted all over, some formal (Palais-Royal, Tuileries), others less so (Parc Montsouris, Bois de Boulogne).

BOIS DE BOULOGNE★★

Ⓜ *Porte Maillot, Sablons (both line 1), Porte d'Auteuil (line 10). RER: Porte Maillot (line C). Buses: 43, 52, 63, 73, 82. Open 24hr all year round. No charge.*

This vast wooded park of 2,100 acres/849ha, once a royal forest, was given to the city by Napoléon III in 1852. Not content with just stamping his mark on the streets of the city, Baron Haussmann landscaped the *bois*, crisscrossing it with wide shaded roads and tracks for pedestrians, horses, and cyclists, and studding it with ornamental lakes and waterfalls, gardens, and lawns. Horse races take place at the Longchamp and Auteuil courses in the park, and music concerts in the Bagatelle and Pré Catelan gardens—two of the three smaller parks within the vast Bois. Visit the park on a weekday morning if you prefer to avoid the weekends, which can get very busy. There are cafés and restaurants if you need a break.

Don't miss:

♦ **The Lakes★** The **Lac Supérieur** is a pleasant recreation area, as is the larger **Lac Inférieur**. There is a motorboat to the islands or you can hire a row boat.

♦ **Pré Catelan★** This well-kept park is named after a court

minstrel from Provence who was murdered here. It includes a luxurious café-restaurant, lawns, and a copper-beech tree that is

BOIS DE BOULOGNE

nearly 200 years old and boasts the broadest spread of branches in Paris.

♦ **Jardin d'Acclimatation**
01 40 67 90 82. www.jardindac climatation.fr. Open daily May–Sept 10am–7pm; Oct–Apr 10am–6pm. 3€. Primarily laid out as a children's amusement park, there's a small zoo with a pets' corner, an "enchanted river",

distorting mirrors, etc., and sports facilities such as a golf driving range for adults.
(See For Kids)

♦ **Parc de Bagatelle★★** *01 40 71 75 60. Open daily Jun–Sept 9.30am–7pm (Oct–Dec & Mar–May 6pm; Jan–Feb 5pm). 5.50€.* In 1775 the future Charles X had a bet with his sister-in-law, Marie-Antoinette, that within

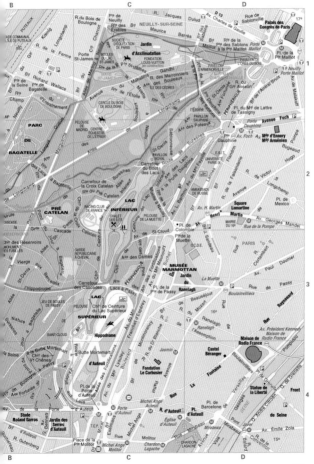

three months he would have a house designed and built, complete with its landscaped garden. He won, and the resulting Bagatelle house and gardens were eventually sold to the City of Paris in 1905. They are now famous particularly for the rose beds, where an annual competition is held, and the water lily pool.

JARDIN DU LUXEMBOURG★★

Ⓜ *Odéon (lines 4 and 10).
RER: Luxembourg (line B). Palais du Luxembourg, rue de Vaugirard. 01 42 34 20 00. Open daily 7.30am–9.30pm (summer); 8.15am–4.30pm (winter). No charge.*
It was Napoléon I who decreed that the gardens of the **Palais de Luxembourg**★★ (which now houses the French Senate) should be dedicated to children, and while the gardens have much to offer visitors of all ages, they do still draw many young mothers or nannies with children, who stop to watch **tennis** or **boules**, to see the **marionnette** (puppet) shows or listen to free concerts, to sail toy boats, or ride miniature ponies. The gardens have a formal layout, except on the west and south sides, where they have the gentler lines of the English style. There are about a hundred **statues and monuments**, commemorating among others the queens of France and other illustrious women. The celebrated **Medici Fountain** (1624, Italian influence) has a lovely shaded setting among plane trees.

JARDIN DU PALAIS-ROYAL★★

Ⓜ *Palais Royal–Musee du Louvre (lines 1 and 7). Bus: 21, 27, 39, 48, 69, 72, 81, 95 and Balabus. www.monuments-nationaux.fr. Open daily, Apr–May 7am–10.15pm; Jun–Aug 7am–11pm; Sept 7am–9.30pm; Oct–Mar 7.30am–8.30pm. Open most public holidays. No charge.*
This quiet formal garden in central Paris now includes modern sculpture installations, and yet retains its 18C atmosphere. The lawns, fountain, and formal avenues of trees are surrounded by galleries of antique shops and high-end fashion boutiques.

Jardin du Luxembourg

Jardin des Plantes

JARDIN DES PLANTES★★

Ⓜ/RER: Gare d'Austerlitz (lines 5 and 10/C). Bus: 24, 57, 61, 63, 67, 89, 91. Place Valhubert. 01 40 79 56 01. www.jardindesplantes.net. Open daily 7.30am–7.45pm (summer); 8am–5.30pm (winter). Main gardens no charge, Jardin Alpin 2€ on weekends, Les Grandes Serres 6€.

The Jardin des Plantes complex includes the Botanical Gardens, the Natural History Museum, and various other study collections of minerals and fossils. It was founded in 1626 by two physicians to Louis XIII, and has been open to the public since 1640. It now encompasses schools for botany, natural history, and pharmacy. The gardens' heyday came when the curator was the **Comte de Buffon** (1707–88), who wrote his 36-volume *Natural History* and still had the time and energy to extend the gardens to the banks of the Seine, plant avenues of lime trees and the **maze**, and build the amphitheater and galleries.

Highlights:

♦ **Botanic gardens** A small gazebo at the highest point gives an overview of the gardens. The famous cedar of Lebanon is one of two planted by Bernard de Jussieu in 1734; legend has it that he carried the plants in his hat after dropping and breaking the pots on his way back from Kew Gardens in England! One of the oldest trees in Paris is a Robinia, or false acacia, planted here in 1636, near the allée des Becquerel.

♦ **Les Grandes Serres** (hothouses) *Open Wed–Mon Oct–Mar 10am–5pm; Apr–Sept 10am–6pm (Sun 6.30pm).* The winter garden glasshouses contain a collection of tropical plants, while the Australian hothouse holds Mediterranean and Australian species, and the Mexican hothouse specializes in cacti.

♦ **School of Botany** *Open daily 8am–7.30pm. Closed public holidays.* Here in the botanical study beds, more than 10,000 species of flora and edible and/or medicinal herbs are classified by family. The **Jardin Alpin** *(open Apr–Oct Mon–Fri 8am–6pm, Sat–Sun 1.30–6pm)* groups its high-altitude plants by soil type and orientation of the sun: Corsica, Morocco (south face), the Alps and the Himalayas (north face). There is also a garden with 180 varieties of antique and hybrid roses, and a walled iris garden combined with perennial and climbing plants.

PARKS AND GARDENS

97

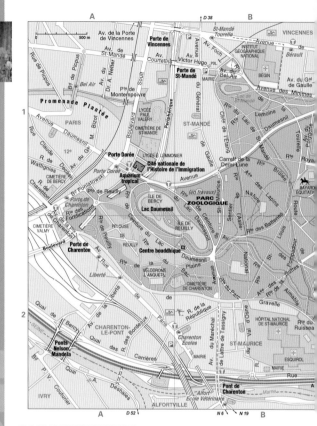

BOIS DE VINCENNES★★

🚇 *Château de Vincennes (line 1), Porte Dorée (line 8). RER: Vincennes (line A). Buses: 56, 325. 01 40 71 74 00. www.boisdevincennes.com. Open daily. No charge.*

Vincennes is known for its château, zoo, lakes, racecourse, beautiful flower garden, and its vast woodland. Originally a royal hunting ground, Napoléon III ceded it (without the château) to the City of Paris in 1860, as an English-style park based on London's Hyde Park.

Highlights:

♦ **Château de Vincennes** *01 48 08 31 20. Visit by guided tour only. www.chateau-vincennes.fr. Open daily mid-May–mid-Sept 10am–6pm; mid-Sept–mid-May 10am–5pm. Chapel open 11am–noon and 3–4pm. Closed public holidays. Tours 8.50€.* Originally a royal residence, parts of the building date back to the Middle Ages. It was later used as an arsenal and a fortress. The impressive **Donjon★★** (keep, 1337) has a 170ft/52m tower enclosed by a fortified

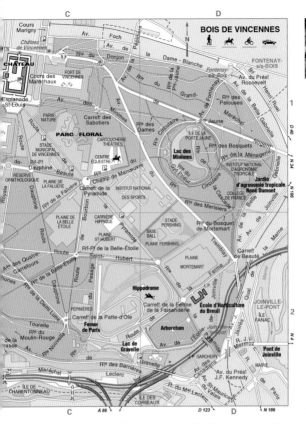

wall and a moat. Henry V of England, died of dysentery here in 1422, and in 1660 Louis XIV spent his honeymoon in the King's Pavilion. State prisoners it has held include the Great Condé, Fouquet (guarded by the "musketeer" d'Artagnan), and authors Diderot and Mirabeau.

♦ **The Park** A very pleasant place to stroll after taking in the history of the château, the large park has various lakes, including the **Lac Daumesnil★**, the **Lac des Minimes**, and the **Lac de Gravelle**. The islands in the

middle of the Lac Daumesnil can be reached by a bridge from the southern bank. The **Île de Reuilly** has a café on it and the **Île de la Porte Jaune** a restaurant. Boats can be hired on both the Lac Daumesnil and the Lac des Minimes. Other attractions include a Buddhist temple, a puppet theater, and the Georges-Ville Farm.

♦ **Le parc zoologique de Vincennes★★** Hundreds of animals and birds can be seen here in the Paris Zoo in natural surroundings. *(See For Kids)*

- **Parc Floral★★** *www.parcfloral deparis.com. Open daily Jan 9.30am–5pm; Feb 9.30am–6pm; Mar 9am–7pm; Apr–Sept 9.30am–8pm; Oct–Dec 9.30am–6.30pm. 3€.* This extensive garden (75 acres/30ha) includes the **Vallée des Fleurs**, which is delightful all year round, its alleyways lined with modern sculpture, and also the **Dahlia Garden**, the **Water Garden**, and a **Four Seasons Garden**.

- **Palais de la Porte Dorée★★** *01 53 59 58 60. www.palais-port edoree.fr. Open Tue–Fri 10am–5.30pm, Sat–Sun 10am–7pm. 8€.* This Art Deco monument houses a tropical aquarium and a museum of the history of Immigration.

BUTTES-CHAUMONT★

Ⓜ *Buttes-Chaumont, Botzaris (both line 7 bis). Buses: 26, 60, 75. Rue Botzaris, between La Villette and Belleville. Open daily May–Sept 7am–10pm; Oct–Apr 7am–9pm. No charge.*

This used to be a sinister area of quarries and rubbish dumps until Napoléon III had Haussmann transform the area into the very first park on the northern edge of Paris, between 1864 and 1867. **The park★** is known for its dramatic hills and cliffs. In the center is a manmade lake, landscaped with huge rocks 164ft/50m high—half natural, half artificial—and an island accessed by two bridges. There is a good view over Montmartre and St-Denis from the Corinthian-style Sybille temple on the island (modeled on the Roman temple of the same name in Tivoli, Italy). Other features include a waterfall and a cave

encrusted with stalactites. There are 3mi/5km of walks, among lawns and trees both indigenous and exotic, including Cedars of Lebanon, the Byzantine Hazelnut, and Siberian Elm.

PARC MONCEAU★

Ⓜ *Monceau (line 2). Main entrance on N side on blvd de Courcelles. 01 47 63 40 90. Open Mon–Fri dawn–dusk, including some public holidays. No charge.*

If you like to pick up on historical resonance, the Parc Monceau (20.3 acres/8.2ha) is for you. It was begun in 1769 by an aristocrat who was later guillotined in the Revolution, and in 1797 it saw the first ever descent by silk parachute, from a hot-air balloon. Ten years after becoming a public park in 1861, it witnessed a massacre of Commune activists. Parc Monceau is now an informal garden in the English manner, dotted with **follies** (in Egyptian, Chinese, Dutch, and Ancient Greek styles), while at the main entrance on the north side is an elegant **rotunda** that was once a tollhouse and is now home to the park keeper. There are play areas for children.

PARC MONTSOURIS★

Ⓜ *Porte d'Orléans (line 4). RER: Cité Universitaire (line B). Buses: 21, 67, 88. Open Mon–Fri 8am–9.30pm (Nov–Mar 8pm), Sat–Sun 9am–9.30pm (Nov–Mar 8pm). No charge.*

The Montsouris Park provides southeast Paris with a real haven of peace, with a lake, lawns, century-old trees, and colorful flowerbeds. Created in 1868–78 in the English style, it has paths that snake up mounds and circle cascades, and a

Statue by Aristide Maillol, Jardin des Tuileries

© Bruce Bi / age fotostock

large artificial lake (which suddenly emptied on opening day, causing the engineer involved to commit suicide). It is decorated with sculptures, including an obelisk that originally marked the Paris meridian. Paris's meteorological observatory is also here. For children there are play areas and pony rides, and a puppet theater.

JARDIN DES TUILERIES★

Ⓜ *Tuileries (lines 1 and 7). RER: Musée d'Orsay (line C). Buses: 42, 68, 72, 73, 84, 94. 01 40 20 90 43. www.louvre.fr/en/departments/ tuileries-and-carrousel-gardens. Open Apr–May & Sept 7am–9pm, Jun–Aug 7am–11pm, Oct–Mar 7.30am–7.30pm. No charge.*
The area now occupied by the Tuileries Gardens has witnessed some of the most turbulent events in the history of Paris. A château was begun here in 1563 for Catherine de' Medici, but it had a checkered history, being abandoned and reduced to a concert hall in the 18C, invaded by revolutionary mobs in 1789 and 1792, revived by Napoléon I, and

finally burned down during the Commune disturbances in 1871.

The layout – The gardens you see today are in the formal French style with lawns, flowerbeds, fountains, and tree-lined gravel walkways. The terraces on either side date back to the 1660s. From the **central walkway** there is a superb **vista★★★** through to the place de la Concorde in one direction and to the Louvre in the other. There are also two cafés and a large play area for kids.

Sculpture and recent changes – Many contemporary sculptures have been placed here in the last 50 years, and since 2000 the gardens have undergone a restoration program. Look out for the fine collection of **nudes★** by **Maillol** in the adjacent Jardin du Carrousel. Steps and ramps provide access at several points to the terraces that run the length of the gardens and end in the **Jeu de Paume** and **l'Orangerie** pavilions *(see Great Galleries).*

101

EXCURSIONS

There are plenty of great options for a day trip. Top of the list may well be Versailles, but what about Monet's gardens at Giverny, or Disneyland Resort to treat the kids? Here are some ideas.

CHÂTEAU DE CHANTILLY★★★

25mi/40km N of Paris in town of Chantilly. 03 44 67 37 37. www.chantilly-tourisme.com.
The Château of Chantilly has links with historical figures such as Henri IV and the Princes of Condé, who were descended from 16C Huguenot leader Louis de Bourbon. There have been castles here for 2,000 years; much of the present one was built in the 1870s, though part dates back to c 1560.

Château★★★

03 44 27 31 80. www.chateaude chantilly.com. Open Apr–Oct daily 10am–6pm (park 8pm); Nov–Mar daily 10.30am–5pm (park 6pm). Château, Musée Conde, & park 14€, Domain pass to include Stables 20€, park & gardens only 7€.
Don't miss:

◆ **Appartements des Princes★** (within the **Petit Château**). Living quarters of the Great Condé and his many descendants: **Chambre de Monsieur le Prince**, the prince in question being the Duke of Bourbon (1692–1740). **Cabinet d'Angles**, a room decorated in white and gold, with 18C furnishings and paintings. **Salon des Singes** decorated with 18C monkey scenes—note the fire screen showing the monkeys' reading lesson. **Galerie de Monsieur le Prince**—the Great Condé ordered a sequence of paintings of military action

(1692), but never saw them completed. The Duke of Aumale had painter Eugène Lami design the **Petits Appartements★** for his marriage in 1844. The opulent rooms give onto a balcony on the ground floor of the Petit Château.

◆ **Chapelle** Well worth seeing are the **Altar★** attributed to Jean Goujon, the 16C marquetry paneling, and stained-glass windows. The **Mausoleum** of Henri II de Condé is in the apse, with bronze statues and a stone urn where the hearts of the Condé princes were placed.

MUSÉE CONDÉ, (GRAND CHÂTEAU)★★

Galerie de Peinture – The feast of paintings includes military works by Neuville and Meissonnier, Orientalism from the brushes of Gros, Vernet, and Fromentin, religious art by Poussin, and historical portraits of Cardinals Richelieu and Mazarin. In the **Santuario★★★** the three Raphaels are unmissable, especially *The Three Graces*. See priceless manuscripts in the **Cabinet des Livres★** (library), including a facsimile of "The Rich Hours of the Duke of Berry," with its stunning 15C illuminations.

Park and Gardens★★

The beautiful grounds designed by LeNôtre include formal French parterres, water features, an English landscaped garden, and a thatched-roof hamlet that inspired Marie-Antoinette's in Versailles.

Grandes Écuries★★ (Stables) and Musée du Cheval ★★

03 44 27 31 80. www.domainede chantilly.com. Open Jan–Mar 2–5pm; Apr–Oct 10am–6pm; Dec 2–6pm. Closed Nov. 11€, with equestrian show 21€.

The stables are Chantilly's most stunning piece of 18C architecture, housing the completely remodelled museum illustrating the history of the horse in art, literature and sports. But the stars of this "living museum" are the French and Spanish horses and ponies inside. If you visit on a special show day there will be an equestrian demonstration to watch.

Forêt de Chantilly

A vast wooded area originally used as hunting grounds, now offering country walks and horse riding.

CHARTRES★★★

57mi/91km SW of Paris. 02 37 18 26 26. www.chartres-tourisme.com.
The town is primarily known for its cathedral, but while you are here take a stroll around the **Old Town★** to see the Romanesque **Église St-André** and walk by the river. In the center of town have a drink in the pretty **place du Cygne**, and see 12C and 13C **Église St-Pierre★**, the monument to resistance fighter **Jean Moulin**, and the 12C half-timbered barn **Grenier de Loëns**.

🏛 Cathedral★★★

02 37 21 75 02. www.cathedrale-chartres.org. Open daily 8.30am–7.30pm (Jul-Aug until 10pm Tue, Fri and Sun).

The cathedral of Notre-Dame in Chartres is acknowledged to be one of Europe's finest medieval buildings and is deservedly a UNESCO World Heritage Site. The finest medieval craftsmen spent their working lives producing its 4,000 statues and the 5,000 figures in its stained-glass windows. The present Notre-Dame was built over the earlier Romanesque cathedral (11C–12C), of which you can still see the crypt, the west front with its towers and Royal Doorway, and fragments of stained glass. The rest was built after a fire of 1194—and in just 45 years. The architecture and decoration have

Chartres Cathedral

EXCURSIONS

Notre-Dame-de-la-Belle-Verrière

a harmony almost unparalleled in Gothic art, left miraculously undamaged by war.

What's outside?

♦ The two spires and Royal Doorway of the **West Front** together form a perfect gem of French religious art (12C). Look up to see the rose window (13C) and gable with the King's Gallery of statues (14C). On the Old Bell Tower, look for the statue of a donkey playing the fiddle, and the tall sundial Angel at the corner.

♦ **Royal Doorway★★★** (*Portail Royal*, Late Romanesque, 1145–70). The doorway is world famous, with its depiction of Christ in Majesty on the central tympanum and gable with its statue-columns of biblical figures at the sides, with their stiff, stylized bodies but animated faces.

♦ **East End** Note the complexity of double-course flying buttresses that soar over the radiating chapels, the chancel, and the transepts.

♦ **Access to the Bell Tower★**
For access times check 02 37 21

22 07 *or www.cathedrale-chartres. monuments-nationaux.fr. 7.50€.* The tour *(195 steps)* leads around the north side and up to the New Bell Tower's lower platform. Seen from a height of 230ft/70m, the flying buttresses, statues, gargoyles, and Old Bell Tower are even more imposing.

What's inside?

♦ **The nave** (13C) is the widest in France, at 52ft/16m. Note how the floor gently slopes up toward the altar, making it easier to wash down after pilgrims had stayed overnight. The chancel and transept are even wider, to cater for huge medieval ceremonies.

♦ **Stained-glass windows★★★** Notre-Dame's glorious windows (12C and 13C) form the largest collection of stained glass in France. Feast your eyes on the famous 12C "Chartres blue," which makes it glow with special radiance in the setting sun.

♦ **West Front** In the three tall windows the scenes illustrate: The Tree of Jesse *(right)*, The Life of Christ *(center)*, and the Passion and Resurrection *(left)*. The large 13C rose window above depicts the Last Judgment, Christ surrounded by 12 Apostles.

♦ **Transepts** Each transept has a 13C rose window above lancet windows. The figures include the Virgin and Child, St Anne holding the infant Virgin Mary, the risen Christ surrounded by the Old Men of the Apocalypse, and four Old Testament prophets, each bearing an Evangelist on his shoulders.

♦ **Notre-Dame-de-la-Belle-Verrière★** A renowned

depiction of the Virgin and Child, it was spared in the fire of 1194 and restored in the 13C.

- **Parclose★★** The screen was started in 1514 and finished only in the 18C. Its 41 sculpted Renaissance medallions depict the lives of Jesus Christ and the Virgin Mary.
- **Chapelle des Martyrs** Now refurbished, this contains the **Virgin Mary's Veil** in a beautiful glass-fronted reliquary with golden angels on either side.
- **Crypt★** *Guided tours (in French only; 30min) 3€. 02 37 21 75 02. Access from outside the cathedral on S side.* This, France's longest crypt (722ft /220m, largely 11C) features Romanesque groined vaulting and has a curious shape with seven radiating chapels, some Romanesque and others Gothic. Look into **St Martin's Chapel** to see the original statues from the Royal Doorway.

DISNEYLAND RESORT PARIS★★★

Located 18mi /30km E of Paris at Chessy. www.disneylandparis.com. Opened in 1992 under the name Euro Disney, **Disneyland Paris** is a vast (over 135 acres/55ha) holiday resort outside Paris with all the facilities and exciting rides you'd expect, and much, much more. It is Europe's biggest visitor attraction, drawing 15 million visitors annually.

Disneyland Park★★★

www.dlrpmagic.com. Disneyland: Open daily Jul–Aug 10am–11pm; Sept–Jun 10am–7pm (out of high season closing times vary). High season 1 day/1 park: 64€ (children 3–11 years 58€); 2 Day/2 Park Hopper tickets also available. Disneyland Paris comprises five "lands," each with a different theme. If you've been to one of the American versions, you will know what to expect—a magical place for both children and adults, and where the latter can forget all about the daily grind for the day. Additionally there's a daily **Disney Parade★★** with all the favorite cartoon characters, and on some evenings the **Main Street Electrical Parade★★** adds the magic of illuminations to the fairytale setting.

Disneyland Resort Paris

© Tim Oram / age fotostock

The five "lands"

Main Street USA – An American town at the turn of the 20C, with period vehicles, musicians, and the **Euro Disneyland Railroad★**, taking you on a ride across the park and through the **Grand Canyon Diorama**.

Frontierland – The Old West, with a typical frontier town, two handsome **steamboats★**, the gold mine in **Big Thunder Mountain★★★** visited by rail (a thrilling runaway train ride), **Phantom Manor★★★** full of mischievous ghosts, and the **Lucky Nugget Saloon★**.

Adventureland – Exciting adventure including **Pirates of the Caribbean★★★**, **Indiana Jones et le Temple du Péril★★★**, and **La Cabane des Robinson★★**—the giant tree-home of the shipwrecked "Swiss family Robinson."

Fantasyland – Centers on Disney's trademark, the dreaming turrets of **Le Château de la Belle au bois dormant★★** (Sleeping Beauty's castle), with also **It's a Small World★★** (a boat ride celebrating childhood, accompanied by an insidiously catchy song), **Alice's Curious Labyrinth★**, **Peter Pan's Flight★★**, **Pinocchio★**, and the dwarfs' mine with **Blanche-Neige et les Sept Nains★** (Snow White and the Seven Dwarfs).

Discoveryland – The world of past discoveries and future dreams: Jules Verne's **Space Mountain★★★** – **De la Terre à la Lune**, also **Star Tours★★★** (interplanetary experience with special effects inspired by *Star Wars*), the famous shrinking machine in **Honey I Shrunk the Audience★★**, and **Le Visionarium★★**, the wonders of Europe on a 360° screen.

Walt Disney Studios Park

Open daily 10am–7pm.
Added in 2002, this offers a trip backstage to discover the secrets of film, animation, and TV.

Front Lot – This is where **Disney Studio 1** reconstructs the film set for **Hollywood Boulevard**.

Toon Studio – **Cinémagique★★★** takes you through the screen to become the film's hero, the **Art of Disney Animation★★** explains Disney's cartoon techniques, while **Animagique★★★** celebrates his full-length animation films. For thrills hop aboard with Aladdin's Genie in **Flying Carpets★**, ride the crazy currents with Nemo in the spinning turtle shell of **Crush's Coaster★★★**, or get the feel of being a tiny toy in **Toy Story Playland★★★** with Toy Soldier Parachute Drop or Slinky Dog's Zigzag Spin. The new **Ratatouille adventure** will be open in late 2014.

Production Courtyard – See what happens backstage in cinema and TV studios. **Cinémagique**★★★ takes you through the screen to become the film's hero. Take a **Television Production Tour**★★ of Disney Channel France. The **Studio Tram Tour**★★ takes you through amazing film sets, while the haunted elevator of the abandoned 1950s Hollywood Hotel in the **Twilight Zone Tower of Terror**★★★ will give you amazing views… and take your breath away!

Disney Village★

Situated beside the theme parks and the lake, in this American town it's always party time. On summer evenings, after the parks close, there is plenty going on here, including **La Légende de Buffalo Bill**★★, an action-filled dinner show complete with horses, buffalo, cowboys, and Indians.

CHÂTEAU DE FONTAINEBLEAU★★★

37mi/60km SE of Paris. 60 74 99 99. www.fontainebleau-tourisme.com.
The spectacular palace you see today was begun in the mid-16C by King François I, after he had

the preceding medieval buildings pulled down, and developed by his descendants through to Louis XVI. It was a favorite residence of Napoléon, and was the scene of his abdication.

Château★★★

01 60 71 50 70. www.musee-chateau-fontainebleau.fr. Open Apr–Sept Wed–Mon 9.30am–6pm (Oct–Mar 5pm). Closed Jan 1, May 1, Dec 25. Grands Appartements & Musée Napoléon I 1€, Petits Appartements 6.50€.
Once used for parades and tournaments, the **Cour du Cheval Blanc** or **Cour des Adieux**★★ got its later name, the Court of Farewells, when Napoléon made his moving speech to the Imperial Guard here after abdicating in April 1814. He was then exiled to the island of Elba.

Grands Appartements★★★

The **Galerie de François I**★★★ was begun in 1528–30, and you can still see François I's monogram and salamander emblem. The **Escalier du Roi**★★ (king's staircase) has murals telling the story of

Grands Appartements, Fontainebleau

© Bertrand Rieger / hemis.fr

EXCURSIONS

Alexander the Great. In the **Salle de Bal★★★** (ballroom), the frescoes and paintings, grand fireplace, and the marquetry floor are simply stunning—as is the spectacular coffered ceiling, rich with silver and gold.

Appartements Royaux★★

The **Salle du Trône** was the king's bedroom from Henri IV to Louis XVI; it was Napoléon who converted it into the throne room. Napoléon also installed his suite **Appartement Intérieur de l'Empereur★**. The **Salon de l'Abdication** is said to be where he signed the abdication document, and the Empire-style furniture dates from that momentous time. A full-length portrait of Louis XIII hangs above the fireplace.

Musée Napoléon I★

Dedicated to the Emperor and his family, the museum holds paintings, sculpture, silverware, medals, ceramics, coronation robes, uniforms, arms, and personal memorabilia.

Petits Appartements

These rooms on the ground floor include the **Petits Appartements de Napoléon I**, and the **Appartements de l'Impératrice Joséphine★**, designed for his wife in 1808. The **Salon Jaune** is one of Fontainebleau's most perfect examples of Empire decoration.

BASILIQUE SAINT-DENIS★★★

In the northern suburbs of Paris. 01 48 09 83 54. www.saint-denis. monuments-nationaux.fr. Open Apr–Sept Mon–Sat 10am–6.15pm (Oct–Mar 5pm), Sun noon–6.15pm (Oct–Mar 5.15pm), last admission 30min before closing. Closed Jan 1, May 1 & Dec 25. 7.50€.

The Basilica was built on the burial place of St Denis, martyred in about AD 250. A succession of churches and abbeys has stood here since AD 475; the one we see today has a unity of design that had a huge influence on late 12C cathedrals and the evolution of the Gothic style. Later falling into disrepair and then ravaged during the Revolution, it was restored in the 19C, chiefly by architect **Viollet-le-Duc**.

What's outside?

◆ The north tower's absence does mar the harmony of the west front, but the double flying buttresses supporting the north side of the nave help to compensate for this lack.

What's inside?

◆ **Mausoleum for the kings of France** For over 12 centuries, all but three of the kings of France, from Dagobert I to Louis XVIII, were buried at St-Denis. In 1793 after the Revolution the tombs were opened and the remains thrown into unmarked graves. However, the most precious tombs were salvaged and returned to the basilica in 1816.

◆ **Tombs★★★** Some early effigies are stylized, being made long after the subject's death, but on the tomb of **Isabella of Aragon** and **Philippe III the Bold** (died 1285) you can see an early concern for accurate portraiture and a sense of personality. By the mid-14C, rulers' effigies were truly lifelike, being made during their lifetime—Henri II's widow **Catherine de' Medici** fainted in horror on seeing herself portrayed in death, so she ordered a new effigy showing her asleep; both can be seen here.

◆ **Crypt**★★ Beneath a marble slab lies the burial vault of the Bourbon family, including the remains of **Louis XVI**, **Marie-Antoinette**, and **Louis XVIII**. In 1817 the bones of around 800 members of the French royal family were reburied in a communal grave here.

Saint-Denis

Named after St Denis, patron saint of France and the first bishop of Paris, the town itself dates back to Roman times but was largely redeveloped in the 1970s. Apart from the basilica, its main claim to fame is as the location of the **Stade de France** *(see Sports and Activities)*.

CHÂTEAU DE VERSAILLES★★★

13.6mi/22km SW of Paris. 01 39 24 88 88. www.versailles-tourisme.com. The matchless palace of Versailles was both the residence of the

court and the seat of government from 1682 until the Revolution. If you have only one day here it's best to begin with the spectacular interior of the château and enjoy a leisurely walk in the park and gardens later.

Château★★★

01 30 83 78 00. www.chateauver sailles.fr. Open Apr–Oct Tue–Sun 9am–6.30pm (Nov–Mar 5.30pm). Château only 15€, Passeport ticket to most areas (including guided tours) 18€, on Grandes Eaux Musicales/Jardins Musicaux days 25€.

The grand period of construction ran from 1664 to 1710, in four phases, creating a palace built around three courtyards: the **Cour des Ministres** (Ministers' Court), the **Cour Royale** (Royal Court), and the vast **Cour de Marbre**★★ (Marble Court), with its black and white marble paving, the heart of Louis XIII's château.

Across from the château entrance is the semicircular **Place d'Armes**★★ (military parade), framed by **La Grande Ecurie**★ (Royal Stables), part of which now houses the

Château de Versailles

© Timehacker / Dreamstime.com

EXCURSIONS

Coach Museum, and also the separate **Academy of Equestrian Arts** *(01 39 02 62 75; www.bartabas.fr; open mid-May–early July Thu 10am–noon; stables and morning recital 12€, horse show 25-40€).* Run by the renowned theatrical horse trainer Bartabas; visit the refurbished stables and highly skilled performances of musical dressage.

State Apartments, Chapel, and Opera – The two-story palatine **Chapelle royale★★★** has a notable ceiling, altar, and gilded bronze relief of a Pietà. The **Opéra Royal★★** (open for guided tours only) was inaugurated in 1770 for the marriage celebrations of the future Louis XVI and Marie-Antoinette. Cleverly, for festivals the floor of the stalls and circle could be raised to stage level. The **Grands Appartements★★★** were used by Louis XIV from 1673 to 1682, and he held court here three times a week. The **Galerie des Glaces★★★** (Hall of Mirrors) was Louis XIV's showpiece for receiving foreign rulers—the ceiling by **Le Brun** depicts Louis's life and victories up to 1678. It was here in this room that the German Empire was proclaimed on January 18, 1871, and the **Treaty of Versailles** was signed on June 28, 1919, ending World War I.

Appartement du Roi or Appartement de Louis XIV★★★ (The King's Suite) – The **Chambre du Roi** was Louis XIV's bedroom from 1701, and he died here. It was in the **Salle du Conseil** (Council Chamber), that the momentous decision was taken to participate in the American War of Independence. The nearby **Appartement de la Reine★★** (Queen's Suite) was constructed for Louis XIV's wife, Queen Marie-Thérèse, who died here in 1683.

Appartement intérieur du Roi★★★ (King's Private Suite). – This was Louis XV's retreat from the Court, and it was in the **Chambre à coucher** that he died of smallpox in 1774.

Grand Park and Gardens★★★

Gardens: Open Apr–Oct daily 8am–8.30pm; Nov–Mar daily 8am–6pm. Free access except Apr–Oct Sat & Sun for Grands Eaux Musicales (fountains play at set times, with music) 9€ (with Passeport 25€), Jardins Musicaux (music in gardens) Jul–Sept Tue 8€. Park: Open Apr–Oct daily 7am–8.30pm; Nov–Mar Tue–Sun 8am–6pm. Free access.
Laid out principally in 1660–70, the park and gardens are masterpieces of French landscape design, in which nature is ordered geometrically according to Classical principles. There is a fine view from the **Parterre du Midi★**.

Domaine de Marie-Antoinette★★

01 30 83 78 00. www.chateau versailles.fr. Open Apr–Oct Tue–Sun noon–6.30pm; Nov–Mar Tue–Sun noon–5.30pm Grand Trianon, Petit Trianon, & gardens only. Domaine de Marie-Antoinette only 10€, with Passeport 18€.
Try not to miss the newly renovated **Marie-Antoinette's Estate** on the northern edge of the Grand Park. It began with the **Grand Trianon★★**, built as a personal retreat for Louis XIV in 1687. Next

door is the **Petit Trianon**★★ (1768), where Marie-Antoinette spent much of her time with her children. She had a private theater, a **garden**★ with lakes and follies, and a replica village, **Le Hameau de la Reine**★★, complete with houses with thatched-roofs, farm animals, and mill. This is where she famously played at being a shepherdess, living the simple country life.

MONET'S GARDEN, GIVERNY★

Near Vernon, 46mi/75km NW of Paris. 84 rue Claude Monet, Giverny. 02 32 51 28 21. http://giverny.org/gardens/ fcm/visitgb.htm. Open daily Apr–Oct. 9.30am–6pm. 6€.

These gardens, so famously painted by Claude Monet, are a place of pilgrimage for his admirers. The Impressionist came here in 1883 to paint direct from nature, and created two gardens. Close to the house there is a traditional "Normandy clos" walled garden with fruit and vegetables growing among flowers. Farther away is the Water Garden (accessed via an underground passage) with its tranquil pond and Japanese bridge, familiar worldwide from Monet's series of unforgettable water lily paintings. Flowers bloom in true cottage garden style, from the tulips and daffodils of April to the dahlias of October, and everything from roses and clematis to sunflowers and hollyhocks, and of course the famous water lilies, in between.

Monet's Garden, Giverny

© Anyka / iStockphoto.com

Musée des Impressionnismes Giverny

99 rue Claude Monet, 27620 Giverny. 02 32 51 94 65. http://giverny.org/museums/ impressionism. Open Apr–Oct, daily 10am–6pm. Closed 1 week late Jul. 6.50€, joint ticket with Monet's Garden 12€. No charge 1st Sun of the month.

Replacing the earlier Musée d'Art Américain de Giverny, this museum uses copies of paintings to give a broad view of Impressionism. The surrounding gardens are free to visit, with meadows of wild flowers beyond.

SPORTS AND ACTIVITIES

Paris has several sporting venues that host major events, but if you would like to take part rather than be a spectator, there are a number of activities you can do while on your trip.

SPECTATOR SPORTS

Palais Omnisports Bercy (POPB) – Ⓜ *Bercy, Gare de Lyon. 8 blvd de Bercy. 0892 390 100. www.bercy.fr/alaune*. A multipurpose venue in central Paris, used for concerts as well as tennis, basketball, show jumping, gymnastics, boxing, and many other sports.

Parc des Princes – Ⓜ *Porte d'Auteuil or Porte de Saint Cloud. www.leparcdesprinces.fr*. Built in 1972, this famous venue for soccer and rugby was the national stadium until the Stade de France was opened in 1998.

Roland Garros – Ⓜ *Porte d'Auteuil. 2 ave Gordon Bennett (near S end of Bois de Boulogne). 01 47 43 48 00, 01 47 43 49 56. www.rolandgarros.com*. This tennis stadium, venue of the French Open championship, has a shop, museum, and behind-the-scenes tours of players' lockers and the courts.

Stade de France – Ⓜ *Saint-Denis – Porte de Paris. RER: Saint-Denis. 01 55 93 00 32. www.stadefrance.com*. Opened in 1998, this vast modern stadium is Paris's main venue for soccer and Rugby Union, and also hosts major popular and classical concerts.

Boules

Played informally on an area of gravel or dirt, you may be able to see a game in the **Jardin du Lux-** embourg *(see Parks)* or the **Arènes de Lutèce** *(See p 34)*

Horse racing

There are famous courses at Longchamp and Auteuil *(W side of Bois de Boulogne)* and at Bois de Vincennes; also a short drive from the city at St-Cloud, Chantilly and Maisons Laffitte. See www.france galop.com for race calendars.

Tour de France

The route of this cycle race covering 2,200mi/3,600km is varied each year to give everyone a chance to see the *Maillot Jaune* (Yellow Jersey) streak past at the head of the pack. Since 1975 the last stage has taken place in the Champs-Élysées (late July).

ACTIVITIES

Boat trips

Bateaux-Mouches – Ⓜ*Alma-Marceau. Pont de l'Alma (Right Bank). 01 42 25 96 10, www. bateaux-mouches.fr*. These large glass-topped boats are a great way to see some of the city's famous sights on a round trip from Pont de l'Alma to Notre-Dame.

Batobus – *08 25 05 01 01. www.batobus.com. Mid-Apr–mid-Sept daily 10am–9.30pm, mid-Sept–mid-Apr 10am–7pm*. A water bus service with eight hop-on/hop-off stops on a round trip along both banks between the Eiffel Tower and the Hôtel de Ville.

MUST DO

Canal St-Martin – Ⓜ *Bastille. 01 42 39 15 00. www.canauxrama.com/ e_saint-martin.htm. See p 61 and 69.* Trips up and down the canal between the Port de Plaisance and La Villette, through locks and a tunnel.

Bike and boat hire

Bikes – *www.velib.paris.fr. Buy a 1- or 7-day prepayment card in advance.* Central Paris now has the ⚡Vélib' *(vélo libre)* system. Pick up a bike at one of the self-service racks across the city and return it at the nearest rack to your destination. Bikes can also be hired from *rental companies* and some offer guided bike tours. Take care and wear a cycling helmet if possible.
Paris Vélo Ⓜ *Richard-Lenoir. 22 rue Alphonse-Baudin, 75011. 01 48 87 60 01. www.parisvelosympa. com.* **Paris Bike Tour** Ⓜ *Filles du Calvaire. 38 rue de Saintonge. 01 42 74 22 14. www.parisbiketour.net/uk.*

Boats – Take a boat out on one of the lakes in the **Bois de Boulogne** or the **Bois de Vincennes** *(see Parks and Gardens).*

Roller skating and rollerblading

Pari Roller *Place Raoul Dautr. 01 43 36 89 81.* Join rollerbladers at 10pm on Fridays (unless wet) in front of the Gare Montparnasse (Ⓜ *Montparnasse-Bienvenüe)* for a 3hr rally. Not for beginners.
Rollers et Coquillages Ⓜ *Bastille. 01 44 54 94 42. www.rollers-coquill ages.org.* Sundays at 2pm at Place de la Bastille for 2–3hr rally. Beginners and experienced skaters. Rent equipment at Place de la Bastille.

Rollers Squad Institut (RSI) Ⓜ *Quai de la Gare. 7 rue Jean-Giono. 01 56 61 99 61. www.rsi.asso.fr.* Organized skating tours. Beginners and experienced skaters.

Swimming

It is compulsory to wear a swimming cap and proper swimming trunks or bathing suit. ⚡**Piscine Josephine Baker** – Ⓜ *Quai de la Gare. Quai Francois Mauriac. 01 56 61 96 50.* A modern floating pool in the River Seine (treated water). Main pool, paddling pool, café, gym, and sundeck. **Stade Nautique Georges Vallerey** – Ⓜ *Porte des Lilas. 148 ave Gambetta. 01 40 31 15 20, 01 58 05 02 30. www. paris.fr (then follow tabs).* A large pool with eight lanes and a sliding roof—open-air in good weather. Café and solarium available.

Tennis

Jardin du Luxembourg – Ⓜ *Notre-Dame-des-Champs. Tennis du Luxembourg, 3 rue Guynemer. 01 43 25 79 18. (See p 96)* **Tennis La Faluère** – Ⓜ *Château de Vincennes (a long walk). 113 Route de la Pyramide, in the center of the Bois de Vincennes. 01 43 74 40 93.* Phone to check opening and book a court.

© AlexQ / Fotolia.com

See Paris by bike

FOR KIDS

Whatever your kids' interests, you will find something to keep them amused in Paris, from hands-on multimedia displays to the simple pleasures of a playground or waterpark.

La Géode

Ludmila Galchenkova / Dreamstime.com

CITÉ DES SCIENCES ET DE L'INDUSTRIE★★★

Ⓜ *Porte de la Villette. 30 ave Corentin-Cariou. 01 40 05 80 00. www.cite-sciences.fr. Combined ticket for all the venues available. Closed Jan 1, May 1, Dec 25.*
The interactive complex at the Cité des Sciences et de l'Industrie has some great activities and exhibits for children—and adults needn't feel left out either. *(See map p 80)*

Explora★★

Open Tue–Sun 10am–6pm (Sun 7pm). 9€ (children over 7 yrs 6€).
Explore the worlds of science and technology on levels 1 and 2 with exhibitions, interactive shows, models, and hands-on activities. Topics include the stars and the galaxies in the planetarium, the importance of water and light to the Earth, how the gardens of the future might do without soil,

computer science, earthquakes and volcanoes, the technological challenges of the future, and much more.

🔹 La Géode★★

01 44 84 44 84. www.lageode.fr. Open Tue–Sun 10.30am–8.30pm. 7–12€.
Seeming to float on the water, this shining steel globe, 118ft/36m in diameter, contains a cinema. The movies shown make the most of La Géode's IMAX system with 3D illusions and other visual effects.

L'Argonaute

Open Tue–Sun10am–5.30pm (Sun until 6.30pm). 3€.
Located near the Géode, this French naval submarine was launched on June 29, 1957 at Cherbourg. While in service it traveled 210,000mi/336,000km and was submerged for a total of 32,700 hours.

MUST DO

Cité des Enfants

08 92 69 70 72. Open Tue–Sun, hours change regularly, generally closed at lunch, check the website. 9€. Reservations highly recommended.

Hands-on interactive heaven for 3–5 and 5–12 year-olds that mixes play and experimentation in science and technology. Sessions last 1hr 30min.

Cité de la Musique

Ⓜ *Porte de Pantin. 221 ave Jean Jaurès. 01 44 84 45 00. www.cite delamusique.fr. Open Tue–Sat noon–6pm, Sun 10am–6pm. 9€ (permanent collection: no charge for under 26s).*

Alongside the Paris National Conservatory of Music and Dance and concert hall, the fascinating **Musée de la Musique**★ contains around 900 musical instruments from the 17C to the present.

Musée de la Musique

© Directphoto / age fotostock

Le Simulateur (Cinaxe)

01 44 84 44 84. Open Tue–Sun 11am–1pm, 2–5pm. 4.80€. Children under 4 not allowed, not advisable for pregnant women and heart patients.

Seating up to 60 at a time, the simulator takes you on a realistic five-minute flight through outer space, or a hair-raising drive around a race track.

MUSEUMS AND OTHER ATTRACTIONS

Musée national de la Marine★★

Ⓜ *Trocadéro. 1 place du Trocadéro et du 11 Novembre. 01 53 65 81 32. www.musee-marine.fr. Open Wed–Mon 10am–6pm (Sat–Sun until 7pm). Closed Jan 1, May 1, Dec 25. 8.50€ (under-18s no charge).*

Children will love the display of precise scale models, such as the nuclear submarine *Le Triomphant* (1996) and the aircraft carrier *Charles-de-Gaulle* (1999), in this superb museum of French maritime history.

Le parc zoologique de Vincennes★★

Ⓜ *Porte Dorée. Ave Daumesnil. 01 44 75 20 10. www.parczoo logiquedeparis.fr. Open mid-Mar–mid-Oct Mon–Fri 10am–6pm, Sat–Sun and public vacations 9.30am–7.30pm; mid-Oct–mid-Mar daily 10am–5pm. 22€.*

Completely renovated and reopened in spring 2014, this innovative zoo is divided into five "biozones": Patagonia, Sahel-Sudan, Europe, Amazone-Guyane, and Madagascar.

Musée Grévin★

Ⓜ *Grands Boulevards. 10 blvd Montmartre. 01 47 70 85 85. www.grevin.com. Open daily 10am–6.30pm (Sat–Sun 7pm). 23.50€ (children 6–14 17.50€).*

Over 300 famous French and international figures recreated in wax and a series of scenes from the 20C and history are in the museum founded by the famous caricaturist Alfred Grévin.

A hall of mirrors and live magic entertainment add to the fun.

🪄 Musée de la Magie★
Ⓜ *Saint-Paul. 11 rue Saint-Paul. 01 42 72 13 26. www.museede lamagie.com. Open Wed, Sat–Sun 2–7pm. Check website for additional opening during school vacations. 9€ (children 7€).*
Discover some of the secrets of the mysterious art of magic from the 18C to today in this intriguing museum. The **Musée des Automates** *(combined ticket 12€, child 9€)* on the same site has over 100 working automata set in an atmospheric old building.

Aquaboulevard
Ⓜ *Balard. 4 rue Louis-Armand. 01 40 60 10 00. www.aqua boulevard.fr. Open Mon–Fri 9am–midnight, Sat 8am–midnight, Sun 8am–11pm. Closed two weeks in Jan. 28€ (children 3–11 years 18€).*
This indoor water-world complex, set among trees and greenery, includes a swimming pool with jacuzzi, wave machine, and giant slide. Also available are mini-golf, bowling, tennis and squash courts, a gym, restaurants, and shops.

Les Étoiles du Rex
Ⓜ *Grands-boulevards, Bonne Nouvelle. 1 blvd Poissonnière. 08 92 68 05 96. www.legrandrex.com. Open Wed–Sun 10am–7pm. 11€ (children under 12 9€).*
Find yourself at the heart of the action in a behind-the-scenes 50min interactive tour of France's most famous movie theater (in French only).

Exploradome
Ⓜ *Villejuif L-Aragon. 18 ave Henri Barbusse. 01 43 91 16 20. www. exploradome.com. Open Tue, Thu, Fri 10am–noon and 1.30–7pm, Wed, Sat 10am–6pm; school vacations Mon–Sat 10am–6pm, Sun and public holidays 1–6pm. Closed Jan 1, Aug 15, Dec 25. 6€ (children under 5 4.50€).*
Family fun with interactive and multimedia displays based on science and technology, where "it is forbidden NOT to touch!."

France Miniature
Gare de la Verrière (train from gare Montparnasse). 258 Route du Mesnil, blvd André Malraux, 78990 Elancourt. 01 30 16 16 30. www.franceminiature.fr. Check website for opening times. 20€ (children 4–14 14€).
An amusement park where you can travel through France in miniature—detailed scale models (some animated) recreate the country's major buildings and monuments from Mont-St-Michel to St Tropez. There are also fairground rides and other attractions.

Georges-Ville Farm – Ferme de Paris
Ⓜ *Château de Vincennes. 1 route du Pesage, Bois de Vincennes. 01 43 28 47 63. Open Apr–Sept weekends 1.30–7pm (Jun–Jul Tue–Sun 1.30–7pm), weekends Oct–Mar 1.30–5pm. Free entry.*
A working farm that gives children a fantastic opportunity to see animals at close quarters, and join in farming activities.

MUST DO

Musée des Égouts

M *Alma-Marceau. Entrance at the corner of quai d'Orsay and pont de l'Alma. 01 53 68 27 81. www.paris.fr. Open Oct–Apr Sat–Wed 11am–4pm (May–Sept until 5pm). Closed two weeks in Jan, Jan 1, Dec 25. 4.40€ (children 6–16 years 3.50€).*
A tour of Paris with a difference, via the sewer system, which was built in the 19C and now incorporates 1,305mi/2,100km of underground tunnels.

Musée en Herbe

01 40 67 97 66. www.musee-en-herbe.com. **M** *Les Halles and Palais Royal; 21 rue Hérold; open daily 10am–7pm; guided tour 6€ (children 10€, workshops 10€).*
Art exhibitions and creative workshops are on offer at this museum created specially for children.

🎭 SHOWS

Traditional puppet and circus shows for kids of all ages, usually in French, but thanks to the strong visual aspect, there's still a lot of fun to be had.

Cirque Diana Moreno Bormann – **M** *Porte-de-la-Chapelle. 112 rue de la Haie Coq. 01 64 05 36 25. www. cirque-diana-moreno.com. Mar–Jul Wed, Sat, Sun at 3pm. 10–45€.*

Cirque du Grand-Céleste – **M** *Porte-des-Lilas. 22 rue Paul Meurice. 01 53 19 99 13. Wed and school vacations (except Mon) at 3pm, Sat at 3pm and 8.45pm, Sun at 4pm.*

Cirque d'hiver Bouglione – **M** *Filles-du-Calvaire. 110 rue*

Many Guignol shows are available to attend

© Plus Lee/iStockphoto

Amelot. 01 47 00 28 81. www. cirquedhiver.com. Nov–end Feb. 10–45€.

Guignol Anatole – **M** *Laumière. Parc des Buttes-Chaumont. 01 43 98 10 95. Outdoors theater (mid Mar–end Oct): Wed, Sat, Sun at 3pm and 4.30pm. 3.50€.*

Guignol & Compagnie – **M** *Sablons. Jardin d'acclimatation, Bois de Boulogne. 01 45 01 53 52. www.guignol.fr. Wed, Sat, Sun at 3pm and 4pm. 2.70€ (including park entrance fee).*

Marionnettes des Champs-Élysées – **M** *Champs-Élysées. Rond-Point des Champs-Élysées. 01 42 45 38 30. www.theatre guignol.fr. Wed, Sat, Sun at 3pm, 4pm, and 5pm. 4€.*

Marionnettes du Luxembourg – **M** *Vavin. Jardin du Luxembourg. 01 43 26 46 47. Wed, Sat, Sun at 4pm.*

Marionnettes du parc Georges-Brassens – **M** *Porte de Vanves. Parc Georges-Brassens,*

rue Brancion. 01 48 42 51 80. www.
marionnettes-parc-brassens.fr.
Wed, Sat, Sun at 3pm, 4pm, and
5pm. 4€.

Théâtre Astral – Ⓜ *Château de
Vincennes. Parc floral de Paris,
Bois de Vincennes. 01 43 71 31 10.
www.theatreastral.com. Jul–Sept.
Reservations required. Check the
theater for times. 7.50€.* Mime,
clowns, and music in shows for
3–8-year-olds that do not rely too
heavily on speech.

La Vallée des Fleurs –
Ⓜ *Château de Vincennes. Parc
floral de Paris, Bois de Vincennes.
Park admission covers events.*
Theater, mime, clowns, and
marionettes.

PLAYGROUNDS, PARKS, AND GARDENS

Cathédrale Notre-Dame★★★

Ⓜ *Cité. Square Jean XXIII.
Open daily dawn–dusk.*
In the gardens just behind the
cathedral. Perfect for the kids
after they have been dragged
around the cathedral!

Butterfly Garden★★

Ⓜ *Château de Vincennes. Parc
floral de Paris. Route du champ de
manoeuvre. 01 49 57 24 84.
www.parcfloraldeparis.fr. Open
daily May 12–Oct 12 1.30–5.30pm
(Sat–Sun 6.30pm). 3€.*
Kids will love watching the
butterflies progress from chrysalis
to colorful fluttering creatures in
this specially created garden area.

Jardin du Luxembourg★★

Ⓜ *Odéon, Cluny-La-Sorbonne.
Open daily dawn–dusk.*
Children can watch puppet
shows, listen to free concerts, sail
toy boats on the grand bassin,
and ride miniature ponies, or just
head for the playground where
there is a range of swings.

Châtelet-Hôtel de Ville★

Ⓜ *Hôtel de Ville. Place de l'Hôtel
de Ville.*
An old-fashioned carrousel is
in pride of place on the square
in front of the Hôtel de Ville. In
summer, when Paris Plage is
in place *(see p 119)*, the square
becomes a beach with
volleyball nets.

Jardin Atlantique★

Ⓜ *Gare Montparnasse. (See p 29)*
Discover this garden in a
surprising place on top of the
roof over Montparnasse station.
Laid out to resemble a ship in
parts, there are also elevated
walkways, fountains, and trees.

Jardin des Tuileries★

Ⓜ *Concorde, Tuileries. Rue de
Rivoli. Open daily dawn–dusk.*
Alongside the elegant statues
and fountains are swings,

*Big wheel,
Jardin des Tuileries*

© Mark Kerr / Michelin

carrousels, trampolines and roller-skating areas, horse and donkey riding, and play areas. In summer *(end Jun–end Aug)*, a fun fair is installed here, with a big wheel from which you get a fabulous view out over the rooftops on a clear day.

Parc Georges-Brassens★
Ⓜ *Convention. Open daily dawn to dusk.*
A playground, carrousel, ping-pong tables, and a climbing area can be found in this 19C park dominated by a wooded hill. Adults might be more interested in the vineyard harvested in early October with great fanfare.

Jardin d'Acclimatation
Ⓜ *Porte Maillot. Rue d'Orléans. 01 40 67 90 82. www.jardindacclimatation.fr. Open daily May–Sept 10am–7pm, Oct–Apr 10am–6pm. 3€.*
This amusement park has a wealth of activities, including a little train, rides on an enchanted river, a hall of mirrors, carrousel, a small zoo with a pets' corner, a typical Norman farm and an aviary.

Terrain d'Aventures
Ⓜ *Les Halles. rue Berger. 01 42 36 13 96. Open Tue–Sat 10am–7pm (until 5pm in winter, until 8pm Jun–Jul), Sun 1–7pm.*
Part of the Jardin des Halles, the kid's adventure area for children 7–11 years old has a climbing wall, slides, a trampoline, a panoramic view hill, and a playground. Pick up a free token 20 minutes in advance for an hour's access to the play area.

🏛 Jardin medieval
Ⓜ *Cluny- La Sorbonne. Blvd St-Germain.*
A special area has been set aside for children to learn about plants and their uses in this recreation of a medieval garden near the **Musée national du Moyen Âge★★**. *(See Major Museums).*

Paris Plage
Various areas along the Seine. 8am–midnight.
Paris beaches transform the city from around July 20 for a month each year. Launched in 2002, the scheme is now a fixture of the summer and offers a Seine-side vacation, with sandy beaches, deck chairs, and evening concerts, plus car-free riverside thoroughfares. There are play areas set aside for children, and at Bassin de la Villette kids can also enjoy kayaking and messing about in small boats.

Square René-Le-Gall
The large play area in the square is an ideal place to pause in a tour of **Les Gobelins** *(see p 31).*

Square Willette
A carrousel and playground in the square below the gleaming white **Sacré-Coeur★★** *(see Landmarks).* When the kids have finally had enough you can take the funicular train up the steep hill to the basilica.

FOR KIDS

STAGE AND SCREEN

Theater performances are usually in French, however international films are often shown as VO *(version originale)* in the original language with French subtitles; VF films *(version française)* are dubbed in French. Parisians are avid filmgoers—some of the more interesting venues are detailed here, but you will find movie theaters all over the capital.

Theaters

National theaters

The capital's state theaters stage top-quality productions by classical and contemporary playwrights. They are normally closed in August.

Comédie-Française – Ⓜ *Palais-Royal. Pl Colette. 01 44 58 15 15. www.comedie-francaise.fr. Box office: 11am–1pm daily.* An historic theater founded in 1680 by Louis XIV, offering principally the classics.

Odéon Théâtre de l'Europe – Ⓜ *Odéon. Pl de l'Odéon. 01 44 85 40 40. www.theatre-odeon.fr. Box office: Mon–Sat 11am–6.30pm.* Renowned for staging 20C works such as Samuel Beckett's *Waiting for Godot* and European productions.

Théâtre National de Chaillot – Ⓜ *Trocadéro. 1 pl du Trocadéro. 01 53 65 30 00. www.theatre-chaillot.fr. Box office: Mon–Sat*

Touring Tip

Kiosque Théâtre
Reduced price tickets available on the day of the performance. No credit cards. Ⓜ *Madeleine. Pl de la Madeleine. Open Tue–Sat 12.30–2pm, Sun 12.30–4pm.*

11am–7pm, Sun 1–5pm. Top theater and dance productions.

Théâtre National de la Colline – Ⓜ *Gambetta. 15 rue Malte-Brun. 01 44 62 52 52. www.colline.fr. Box office: Mon–Sat 11am–6.30pm, Sun 1–4.30pm.* Founded in a small street in the east of Paris in 1951, it stages excellent contemporary dramas.

La Cartoucherie Ⓜ *Château de Vincennes. Rte du Champ-de-Manœuvres, Bois de Vincennes. 01 43 74 88 50 or 01 43 74 24 08.* In a peaceful setting in the Bois de Vincennes, the Cartoucherie has five theaters including the Théâtre du Soleil, which enjoys an international reputation.

Théâtre Marigny Ⓜ *Champs-Élysées-Clemenceau. Ave de Marigny. 01 53 96 70 00. www.theatremarigny.fr. Box office: Mon–Sat 11am–6.30pm, Sun 11am–3pm. Closed Jul–Aug.* Just off the Champs-Élysées, Roman

Odéon Théâtre de l'Europe

© Rosine Mazin / Photononstop

MUST DO

BOX OFFICE

Polanski produced *Amadeus* here. The Marigny is known for good modern French drama.

Théâtre Mogador

🚇 *Trinité. 25 rue Mogador. 01 53 32 32 32. www.stage-entertainment.fr/theatre-mogador. Box office: Mon–Sat 10am–7pm, Sun 10am–4pm.*
A good bet for non-French speakers because musicals such as *Mamma Mia!* and *The Lion King* are staged here.

Théâtre du Rond-Point

🚇 *Franklin-D-Roosevelt. 2 bis ave Franklin-Roosevelt. 01 44 95 98 21. www.theatredurondpoint.fr. Box office: Tue–Sat 2–7pm, Sun noon–4pm. Closed summer.*
Repertory and contemporary theater in a building that was once a skating rink.

Cinemas

Cinéma l'Entrepôt

🚇 *Pernety. 9 rue Francis-de-Pressensé. 01 45 40 07 50. www.lentrepot.fr.*
Perfect for film buffs with films in VO and experimental feature-length cinema, plus weekend concerts. Also a bar and restaurant with a garden terrace.

La Cinémathèque française

🚇 *Bercy. 51 rue de Bercy. 01 71 19 33 33. www.cinematheque francaise.com. Closed Tue.*
With a mission to preserve and restore films, it also shows international classics and holds retrospectives and exhibitions.

©Stéphane Dabrowski / Cinémathèque Française
La Cinémathèque française

Cinéma Le Grand Rex

🚇 *Bonne-Nouvelle. 1 blvd Poissonnière. 08 92 68 05 96. www.legrandrex.com.*
Built in 1932, shows VF box-office-type movies. When you enter, look up at the starry night-sky ceiling above the decorative interior.

Cinéma Mac-Mahon

🚇 *Charles-de-Gaulle-Étoile. 5 ave Mac-Mahon. 01 43 80 24 81. www.cinemamacmahon.com. Closed Aug.*
A shrine to the film goddesses of the 1950s and 60s showing the classics in their original format (VO only) with newsreels of the period.

La Pagode

🚇 *St-François-Xavier. 57 bis rue de Babylone. 09 62 23 05 33.*
In a superb Japanese pagoda, art house and independent films are shown here.

Max Linder Panorama

🚇 *Grands Boulevards. 24 blvd Poissonnière. 08 92 68 00 31. www.maxlinder.cine.allocine.fr.*
Art house and independent films with an accent on culture. One screen; excellent acoustics.

LIVE MUSIC AND DANCE

All kinds of music and dance is available in Paris and at all kinds of venues, from the historic Opéra-Garnier and vast modern arenas such as Zénith to intimate *boîtes de jazz* (clubs). Here are some suggestions.

Classical and contemporary

Casino de Paris
🚇 *Trinité. 16 rue de Clichy. 01 49 95 22 22. www.casinodeparis.fr.*
Among the contemporary stars following in the footsteps of Maurice Chevalier at this historic music hall are Sylvie Vartan and Natalie Cole. Also shows such as *Fame* and *Stomp*.

Châtelet-Théâtre Musical de Paris (TMP)
🚇 *Châtelet. Pl du Châtelet. 01 40 28 28 40. www.chatelet-theatre.com. Box office: 10am–7pm by phone or 11am–7pm at theater.*
A theater with a rich heritage staging top-quality concerts, opera, and dance.

Cité de la Musique
🚇 *Porte de Pantin. 221 ave Jean-Jaurès. 01 44 84 44 84. www.cite-musique.fr. Box office: Tue–Sat noon–6pm, Sun 11am–6pm.*
This state-of-the-art complex includes a concert hall, amphi-theater, and museum of music.

Maison de Radio-France
🚇 *Passy. 116 ave du Prés. Kennedy. 01 56 40 15 16. www.radiofrance.fr.*
Free or inexpensive jazz, classical, and contemporary concerts.

Salle Pleyel
🚇 *Ternes. 252 rue du Fg-St-Honoré. 08 42 56 13 13. www.sallepleyel.fr. Box office: Mon–Sat noon–7pm, Sun from 11am. Closed Jul–Aug.*
Completely renovated in 2006, this Art Deco theater is known for great performances by world-class figures (Casals, Menuhin, Rubinstein).

Théâtre des Champs-Élysées
🚇 *Alma-Marceau. 15 ave Montaigne. 01 49 52 07 41. www.theatrechampselysees.fr. Closed Jul–Aug.*
Choose a traditional evening performance or a Sunday morning concert at this historic theater. Von Karajan, the Bolshoi, the Ballet de Paris, Maurice Béjart, and Josephine Baker, among others, have all played here.

Jazz, blues, and world

Jazz-Club Etoile
🚇 *Porte-Maillot. 81 blvd Gouvion-St-Cyr. 01 40 68 30 42. www.jazzclub-paris.com. Dinner 8.30pm; concerts 9.30pm.*
This dinner club remains true to its jazzy origins. You can count on finding traditional jazz (New Orleans, Swing) concerts, along with real rhythm 'n' blues.

Le New Morning

Ⓜ *Château-d'Eau. 7–9 rue des Petites-Écuries. 01 45 23 51 41. www.newmorning.com. Open 8pm–1am. Closed Aug.*

Jazz, world music, salsa, and blues at this lively eclectic club. Great atmosphere. Arrive early to get a seat.

Le Petit Journal Montparnasse

Ⓜ *Montparnasse-Bienvenüe, Gaîté. 13 rue du Cdt-Mouchotte. 01 43 21 56 70. www.petit-journal. com. Open Mon–Sat 8pm–2am. Concerts: 10pm. Closed mid-Jul– mid-Aug.*

A bastion of jazz, a long line of the greats played here, including Eddy Louiss and Richard Galliano. Mostly modern jazz, with a swing or blues slant.

Sunside Sunset

Ⓜ *Châtelet. 60 rue des Lombards. 01 40 26 46 60. www.sunset-sunside.com.*

An electric jazz hotspot with a little fusion thrown in, featuring international and homegrown artists, downstairs (Sunset).

Opera and Dance

Opéra-Bastille

Ⓜ *Bastille. Pl de la Bastille. 01 40 01 17 89/08 92 89 90 90. www.operadeparis.fr. Box office: Mon–Fri 9am–6pm, Sat 9am– 1pm. Closed mid-Jul–mid-Sept.*

Inaugurated in 1989, the home of the Opéra National de Paris, the modern Opéra-Bastille has become Paris's principal opera venue. Great acoustics and high-tech stage wizardry.

Opéra-Comique (Salle Favart)

Ⓜ *Richelieu-Drouot. 5 rue Favart. 08 25 00 00 58/01 42 44 45 46. www.opera-comique.com. Box office: Mon 9am–2pm, 3.15–6pm, Tue–Sat 9am–9pm, Sun 11am– 3pm, 4.15–7pm. Closed Aug.*

Operas such as Bizet's *Carmen* (1875), Léo Delibes's *Lakmé* (1883), and *Pelléas et Mélisande* all made their débuts at this historic opera house. Today it stages more lightweight productions.

Opéra-Garnier

©PobladuraFCG /iStockphoto.com

LIVE MUSIC AND DANCE

Palais Garnier

M *Opéra. 8 rue Scribe. 01 40 01 18 11/08 36 69 78 68. www.opera deparis.fr. Box office: Mon–Sat 11am–6.30pm. Closed mid-Jul– early Sept.*

Formally inaugurated in 1875, the famous Paris opera house now mainly stages ballet. Hard to beat for sheer *belle époque* exuberance, you can enjoy the surroundings as well as the performance.

Théâtre de la Ville

M *Châtelet. 2 pl du Châtelet. 01 42 74 22 77. www.theatredela ville-paris.com. Box office: Tue–Sat 11am–8pm, Mon 11am–7pm.*

A good venue for ballet, drama, and popular, traditional, and classical music, often showcasing new talent. Once run by Sarah Bernhardt, the theater has acquired a reputation for presenting the work of contemporary choreographers such as Merce Cunningham and Boris Charmatz.

Rock and Pop

Le Bataclan

M *Oberkampf. 50 blvd Voltaire. 01 43 14 00 30. www.le-bataclan.com.*

With performances by LL Cool J, Massive Attack, and the Scissor Sisters, Le Bataclan is a stalwart of the contemporary circuit.

La Cigale

M *Anvers, Pigalle. 120 blvd Rochechouart. 01 49 25 81 75. www.lacigale.fr.*

Since Philippe Starck revamped this historic theater in 1987, Le Cigale has become the home of contemporary rock and pop artists.

Le Trianon

M *Anvers. 80 blvd de Rochechouart. 01 44 92 78 00. www.letrianon.fr. Concerts: 7.30– 10.30pm.*

A historic concert venue completely restored in 2010, with a varied program of French and international musicians such as Texas, Jay Jay Johanson, Rufus Wainwright, and Macy Gray.

Olympia

M *Opéra. 28 blvd des Capucines. 01 47 42 25 49 or 08 92 68 33 68 (reservations by tel). www.olympia hall.com. Concerts: 8.30pm, Sun 5pm. Closed Aug.*

All kinds of performers from Edith Piaf and the Grateful Dead to Madonna have been on stage at this long-established venue.

Palais Omnisports de Paris-Bercy (POPB)

M *Bercy. 8 blvd de Bercy. 08 25 03 00 31. www.bercy.com.*

Concerts by the likes of Lady GaGa, Michael Bublé, and Bruce Springsteen, and major sports events *(see Sports and Activities).*

Zénith

M *Porte de Pantin. 211 ave Jean-Jaurès. 01 42 08 60 00. www.le-zenith.com.*

A vast concert hall at La Villette where just about everyone who is anyone has played, plus shows such as *Holiday on Ice.*

NIGHTLIFE

What could be more Parisian than café-théâtre, mixing humor, song, and satire? If you don't speak French you may feel a little left out, so instead try a cabaret or revue. It's all a bit kitsch, with high-kicking dancers (maybe topless), feathers, glitter, song, and dance, but if you go to one of the better known venues you can be sure of some polished entertainment. Clubbers need not feel left out as there are venues all over the city where you can dance to anything from world music to hip-hop and techno, or just enjoy a cocktail.

Cabarets and Revues

Crazy Horse
Ⓜ *George V. 12 ave George-V. 01 47 23 32 32. www.lecrazy horseparis.com.*
A sparkling evening is in store with dancers in fabulous costumes performing original choreographed set pieces.

🜚 Moulin-Rouge
Ⓜ *Blanche. 82 blvd de Clichy. 01 53 09 82 82. www.moulin-rouge.com. Box office: 9am–1am.*
Immortalized in Toulouse-Lautrec's paintings, the revue is as spectacular as ever with glamorous dancers and singers.

Folies-Bergère
Ⓜ *Cadet, Grands Boulevards. 32 rue Richer. 01 44 79 98 98. www.foliesbergere.com. Box office: 10am–6pm.*
The oldest venue of its kind in Paris, the great Folies-Begère keeps the spirit of Parisian revues burning bright with its splendid shows in an equally splendid setting.

Le Lido
Ⓜ *George V. 116 bis ave des Champs-Élysées. 01 40 76 56 10. www.lido.fr.*
Le Lido is a must for the celebrated Bluebell Girls, founded by an Irish dancer in the 1930s. Over 600 costumes, fountains and other stunning stage effects.

Moulin-Rouge

© Moulin-Rouge®

Nuit Blanche

Every year, on one night in October, the galleries and museums of Paris, along with many other institutions, throw open their doors all night to visitors, with free entry, for a "white night," as the French call a sleepless night. There are shows and concerts, elaborate light displays—plenty to do and see to ensure you won't feel the need to go to bed until dawn breaks over the city, if you're still awake that is.

Le Paradis Latin

Ⓜ *Jussieu, Cardinal Lemoine. 28 rue du Cardinal Lemoine. 01 43 25 28 28. www.paradis-latin.com.*
Gustave Eiffel designed this beautiful old theater staging glittering song and dance shows, for the World Fair in 1889.

Café-théâtres

Le Lapin Agile

Ⓜ *Lamarck-Caulaincourt. 22 rue des Saules. 01 46 06 85 87. www.au-lapin-agile.com. Open Tue–Sun 9pm–1am.*
A famous venue, true to the spirit of the early 20C when Modigliani and Picasso would spend an evening or two here, among the bohemian and sometimes dubious characters who frequented the district. Know for its bawdy songs and political satire (in French).

Les Deux Ânes

Ⓜ *Blanche. 100 blvd de Clichy. 01 46 06 10 26. www.2anes.com. Shows: Tue–Sat 8.30pm, Sat matinee 4.30pm. Closed Jul–Aug.*
Biting satire on current affairs and politics, mixed with traditional French songs.

Clubs

Le Batofar

Ⓜ *Quai de la Gare. Quai François M-Mauriac. 01 71 25 50 61. www. batofar.org. Tue– Sun 8pm–2am.*
A former lighthouse ship, dance below decks to house, trance and techno, and sometimes live bands too. It usually gets pretty busy so you might need to wait in line at weekends.

Charlie Birdy

Ⓜ *Franklin D. Roosevelt, George V. 124 rue de la Boetie. 01 42 25 18 06. www.charliebirdy.com. Tue–Sun 8pm–2am.*
A large lively Anglo-American bar with live jazz and blues at the weekends, sports matches on the big screens, and a long cocktail menu. Relax in one of Charly Birdy's Chesterfields during the week and take advantage of Happy Hour. There are two other Paris branches, in Montparnasse and Commerce.

La Chapelle des Lombards

Ⓜ *Bastille. 19 rue de Lappe. 01 43 57 24 24. www.la-chapelle-des-lombards.com. Wed–Sun 11.30pm–6.00am.*
It's hard to keep still at this dance club playing *musique tropicale*, from salsa and zouk to reggae and r&b, with an emphasis on world music. Smart dress.

La Coupole
🚇 *Vavin. 102 blvd du Montparnasse. 01 43 20 14 20. www.lacoupole-paris.com. Sun 2.30–7pm.*

Upstairs the legendary brasserie, downstairs a dance hall where Josephine Baker once performed, now famous for its Sunday afternoon "thés dansants", ballroom dancing to tango, salsa, swing, cha-cha, fox trot and rumba.

Harry's New York Bar
🚇 *Opéra. 5 rue Daunou. 01 42 61 71 14. www.harrysbar.fr. Noon–2am or later.*

A bar with a history, opened in 1911 at "Sank Roo Doe Noo," as 5 rue Daunou is written phonetically, it was a Hemingway haunt and is still popular with expat Americans. Chic atmosphere and great cocktails. It is said to be the birthplace of the ever popular Bloody Mary.

🍸 Lizard Lounge
🚇 *Hôtel de Ville, St-Paul. 8 rue du Bourg-Tibourg. 01 42 72 81 34. www.cheapblonde.com. Noon–2am.*

Relaxed and intimate, a hip American-style bar with Happy Hour, food is served upstairs and there's a DJ and dancing downstairs.

La Machine
🚇 *Barbès Rochechouart. 90 blvd de Clichy. 01 53 41 88 89. www.la machinedumoulinrouge.com.*

Previously La Loco, and now taken over by the legendary Moulin-Rouge next door, there are three floors of pulsating music and dance in a variety of styles.

Le Queen
🚇 *George V. 102 avenue des Champs-Elysées. 01 53 89 08 90. www.queen.fr.*

A famous club in a famous part of town holding special nights (check the website in advance) and with guest international DJs. With a reputation for celebrity sightings on the large dance floor, it's no surprise to learn that an evening at Le Queen can be expensive.

Rex Club
🚇 *Bonne Nouvelle. 5 blvd Poissonière. 01 42 36 10 96. www.rexclub.com.*

Originally part of the rave scene, the Rex Club has been specializing in electronic music for over 20 years. Today a host of international DJs play nu soul, techno, and electro hip-hop.

Sanz Sans
🚇 *Abbesses. 49 rue du Fg-St-Antoine. 01 44 75 78 78. www.sanzsans.com.*

Kitsch and glitzy décor. The DJ-led music is loud and the crowd congregating around the central bar lively, When very busy they even dance on the bar.

NIGHTLIFE

SHOPPING

One of the best things about shopping abroad is getting away from the familiar names of your own shopping streets and malls and discovering new ones. There is a wealth of different stores and boutiques right across Paris, full of fashions, luxury brands, gourmet produce, antiques, and souvenirs, all just waiting to tempt you. You may need to buy a suitcase to take them all home! *(For the areas that correspond to each arrondissement, see p 154.)*

Galeries Lafayette de Paris

© Kevin Cummins / Apa Publications

Department stores

All stock a wide range of goods, but Printemps and Galeries Lafayette have large clothing departments, BHV is good for home wares, and the exclusive Le Bon Marché has a particularly good food hall.

Galeries Lafayette de Paris – Ⓜ *Chaussée-d'Antin. 40 blvd Haussmann. 01 42 82 34 56. www. galerieslafayette.com. Open daily 9.30am–8pm (Thu 9pm).*

Au Printemps – *RER: Auber. 64 blvd Haussmann. 01 42 82 50 00.www.printemps.fr. Open daily 9.35am–7pm (Thu 10pm).*

Le Bon Marché – Ⓜ *Sèvres- Babylone. 24 rue de Sèvres. 01 44 39 80 00. www.lebonmarche.com.*

Open Mon–Sat 10am–8pm (Thu–Fri 9pm).

BHV (Le Bazar de l'Hôtel - de-Ville) – Ⓜ *Hôtel-de-Ville. 14 rue du Temple. 01 42 74 90 00. www.bhv.fr. Open daily 9.30am–8pm (Wed 9pm).*

Shopping Malls

Carrousel du Louvre – Ⓜ *Palais-Royal. 01 43 16 47 10. Open daily 9.30am–10pm (shops open 10am–8pm).*

Centre commercial Montparnasse – Ⓜ *Montparnasse-Bienvenüe Place du 18-Juin-1940. Open Mon–Sat 10am–8pm.*

MUST DO

Forum des Halles – **Ⓜ** *Les Halles.*
101 Porte Berger. 01 44 76 96 56.
www.forumdeshalles.com. Open
Mon–Sat 10am–8pm.

Bastille★ – Faubourg St-Antoine

11th arrondissement

Furniture and clothes shops
jostle for attention next to art
galleries and artists' studios in the
maze of streets in this area. For
contemporary art head for **rue de
Charonne**, **rue de Lappe**, and **rue
Keller**. Superb wines and expert
advice are available at **Septime
La Cave** *(3 rue Basfroi; 01 43 67 14
87)* and **Des Mets des Vins** *(20 rue
d'Aligre; 01 44 68 22 94).*

Beaubourg★★ – Les Halles

1st–2nd–3rd arrondissements

Place des Innocents, **rue Pierre-
Lescot**, and the narrow streets near
Les Halles—**rue des Prêcheurs** and
rue de la Grande-Truanderie—are
lined with shops selling jewelry,
postcards and posters, shoes, and
clothing. Fashion can be found at
Agnès B *(6 rue du Jour; 01 45 08 56
56)*, and everything for the budding
dress or jewelry maker at **La
Droguerie** *(9–11 rue du Jour; 01 45
08 93 27)*. Fine food stores include
Strohrer *(51 rue Montorgueil; 01 42
33 38 20)* founded in 1730 and now
a listed building. The finest wine
can be found at **Legrand Filles et
Fils** *(1 rue de la Banque; 01 42 60
07 12)*.

Butte-aux-Cailles – Gobelins – Tolbiac

13th arrondissement

The comprehensive wine cellar
Cave des Gobelins *(56 ave des
Gobelins; 01 43 31 66 79)* has some

rare vintage spirits (including a
cognac from 1809!) and practically
every fine wine produced over the
last 40 years. **Les Abeilles** *(21 rue de
la Butte-aux-Cailles; 01 45 81 43 48)*
sells every kind of honey product,
including candies, royal jelly, soap,
beeswax, and honey.

🏛 Champs-Élysées★★★ – La Madeleine★★

8th arrondissement

For luxury brands visit the
Champs-Élysées area. From **Les
Trois Quartiers** *(23 blvd de la
Madeleine; 01 42 97 80 06)* to the
wide avenues of **rue Royale** and
avenue Montaigne, you will find
some of the smartest streets in
Paris with high-end fashion (**Adolfo
Dominguez, Gucci**), jewelry
(**Poiray, Fred**), crystal (**Christofle,
Cristallerie Saint-Louis**), and
china (**Bernardeau**). The legendary
house of **Chanel** is nearby *(31 rue
Cambon; 01 42 86 28 00)* and the
historic perfume store **Guerlain** *(68
ave des Champs-Élysées; 01 45 62
11 21)*. The **Drugstore Publicis** *(133
ave des Champs-Élysées; 01 44 43 79
00)* is a stylish outlet that includes
a café, restaurant, and cinema, as
well as selling luxury gifts, wine,
and books. For exclusive crystal/
glassware try **Baccarat** *(11 place de
la Madeleine; 01 42 65 36 36)* and
Lalique *(11 rue Royale; 01 53 05 12
12)*. **La Ferme La Fontaine** *(75 rue
La-Fontaine; 01 42 88 07 55)* has
been home to five generations of
cheese merchants since 1890, and
🏛**Ladurée** *(75 ave des Champs-
Élysées; 01 40 75 08 75)* offers
exquisite cakes, pastries, and divine
macaroons in 13 flavors. Close by in
place de la Madeleine are **Fauchon**
*(24–30 place de la Madeleine; 01 70
39 38 00)*—a delicatessen, *patissier*,

Label heaven

Paris is bursting at the seams with luxury brands. If your pockets are deep enough, join the label-conscious in the smart streets around the Champs-Élysées and place des Victoires. For alternative trends, explore the fashionable boutiques around rue des Francs-Bourgeois in Le Marais.

high-class grocer, and tea room all rolled into one—and **Hédiard** *(21 place de la Madeleine; 01 43 12 88 88)* renowned for its delicious array of exotic fruits and spices, and fine wine cellar.

Invalides★★★ – Sèvres-Babylone★
7th arrondissement

Visit the streets around **rue du Bac** for inspirational interior-design stores. **Le Cabinet de Porcelaine** *(37 rue de Verneuil; 01 42 60 25 40)* sells superb pieces of antique porcelain. Foodies should visit **Richart** *(258 blvd St-Germain; 01 45 55 66 00)* where the chocolates resemble miniature paintings. **Barthélémy** *(51 rue de Grenelle; 01 45 48 56 75)*, still with its original 1900 decor, is a must for cheese fans, and for the best bread in town stop at **Poilâne** *(8 rue du Cherche-Midi; 01 45 48 42 59)*.

Latin Quarter★★
5th arrondissement

If you are interested in comics *(bandes dessinées)* head for the **rue Dante** where the specialist strip-cartoon dealers are located. The **Maison des trois thés** *(1 rue Saint-Médard)* sells close to 450 teas, including some of the rarest and most expensive. **Shakespeare & Co** is now as much a tourist attraction as an English language bookstore *(37 rue de la Bûcherie; 01 43 26 96 50)*.

Le Marais★★★
4th arrondissement

Explore the streets around **rue des Francs-Bourgeois** for cutting edge fashion. The **Temple** district is good for tailored leather and wholesale jewelry and is also known for its antique and art galleries in **place des Vosges** and **Village St-Paul** *(off rue St-Paul)*. Also home to a large Jewish community, you will find the best in kosher food at **Izrael Épicerie du Monde** *(30 rue François-Miron; 01 42 72 66 23)*, and **Sacha Finkelsztajn** *(27 rue des Rosiers; 01 42 72 78 91)*, a treasure trove of spices, flavors, and delicacies.

Montmartre★★★ – Pigalle
18th arrondissement

South of boulevard de Rochechouart, in the **Goutte-d'Or** district, there's an eclectic range of shops selling Arab and African fabric, luggage, and jewelry. To satisfy a sweet tooth, there's **Arnold Delmontel** *(39 rue des Martyrs; 01 48 78 29 33)*, which sells tasty bread as well as superb pastries, and croissants.

Opéra★★ and Les Grands Boulevards★
2nd–9th–10th arrondissements

This area has a number of well-known food stores: **Furet** *(63 rue de Chabrol; 01 47 70 48 34)* sells legendary **Tanrade** jams; the Algerian pastry store **La Bague de**

Kenza (106 rue St-Maur; 01 43 14 93 15) offers cakes and pastries; while the oldest wine cellar in Paris is **Augé** (116 blvd Haussmann; 01 45 22 16 97). **À la Mère de Famille** (35 rue du Fg-Montmartre; 01 47 70 83 69) is a quaint grocery-cum-candy store.

Palais-Royal★★ – St-Roch
1st arrondissement
Near the Palais-Royal are the elegant window displays of perfumer **Les Salons du Palais-Royal Shisheido** (142 gal. de Valois; 01 49 27 09 09). Around **place des Victoires** are top designers such as **Kenzo** (3 place des Victoires; 01 40 39 72 03) and **Jean-Paul Gaultier** (6 rue Vivienne; 01 42 86 05 05). You'll find smart sportswear and classic clothes at **Ventilo** (27 bis rue du Louvre; 01 44 76 82 97). There are around 250 antique dealers at **Le Louvre des Antiquaires** (2 place du Palais-Royal; 01 42 97 27 27) while on a far smaller scale, you can find a number of antique shops in the **Galerie Véro-Dodat** (see p 45). If you do need that extra suitcase, try the luggage makers **Goyard** (233 rue St-Honoré; 01 42 60 57 04). Follow the delicious smell of freshly ground coffee to **Verlet** (256 rue St-Honoré; 01 42 60 67 39), which has been selling coffee and tea since 1880.

Saint-Germain-des-Prés★★
6th arrondissement
This is where upscale antique shops and galleries meet fashion and food stores. *Traiteurs* and delicatessens can be found around **Carrefour de Buci**. All the well-known couture names are here: **Christian-Lacroix** (2–4 place

St-Sulpice; 01 46 33 48 95), **Yves Saint-Laurent** (6 place St-Sulpice; 01 43 29 43 00). For chocolates and desserts visit **Christian-Constant** (37 rue d'Assas; 01 53 63 15 15) and **Debauve et Gallais** (30 rue des Sts-Pères; 01 45 48 54 67),

Debauve et Gallais
© Debauve et Gallais

once patronized by the kings of France. There's also a number of bookstores, many selling English-language works: **La Hune** (16-18 rue de l'Abbaye, 01 45 48 35 85) and **L'Écume des Pages** (174 blvd St-Germain 01 45 48 54 48); **Gibert Joseph** (26 blvd St-Michel; 0144 41 88 88), also selling stationery and CDs. Visit **rue de Furstemberg** for interior design stores, while **Le Carré Rive Gauche** is an association of some 120 art galleries and antique dealers spread around rue des Saints-Pères, rue de l'Université, and along quai Voltaire.

MARKETS

Unlike many cities, the whole of Paris is very much lived in—including the center—and you will find street markets in many areas selling everything from food to small household goods. In addition to these are the specialist markets such as flea markets.

Marché Belleville

ⓜ *Ménilmontant, Belleville. Blvd de Belleville. Open Tue & Fri 7am–2.30pm.*

Spreading for blocks, this market is full of good buys on ethnic foods, spices, and a broad variety of other goods. This is one of the largest outdoor markets in Paris and you can spend several happy hours just looking round all the stalls.

Marché Biologique Raspail

ⓜ *Notre-Dame des Champs. Blvd Raspail. Open Sun am.*

Come here for a tempting selection of organic fruit, vegetables, cheeses, and wine, along with fresh bread and raw chocolate. Rendezvous for the trendy locals; quite pricey but interesting.

Marché les Enfants Rouges

ⓜ *Filles-du-Calvaire. 39 rue de Bretagne. Open Tue–Fri 9am–2pm, 4–8pm, Sat 9am–8pm, Sun 9am–2pm.*

Hidden away in the North Marais quarter, this market founded in the early 17C (named after an orphanage whose children were dressed in red) was completely rebuilt in 2000 and is now a trendy lunch venue.

Marché aux Fleurs et aux Oiseaux

ⓜ *Cité. Place Louis-Lepine. Open daily 8am–7.30pm.*

This is one of the last Parisian markets dedicated to plants, some rare and specialized, and birds (on a Sunday). It has been operating

Marché aux fleurs

© S.Sauvignier / Michelin

Bargain hunting at flea market, Marché aux Puces

for over 200 years and is a bucolic, colorful oasis far from the madding crowds at Notre-Dame nearby.

Marché du Livre Ancien et d'Occasion

M Convention, Porte de Vanves. Rue des Morillons. Open Sat & Sun 9am–6pm.

Around 60 to 80 *bouquinistes* (book dealers) sell their literary wares every weekend inside a covered pavilion beside Parc Georges Brassens.

Marché Maubert

M Maubert-Mutualité. Place Maubert. Open Tue & Thu 7am–2.30pm, Sat 7am–3pm.

A wide selection of cheese, dairy products, meats, flowers, fruit, pastries, and nonedibles, such as paper and household goods.

Marché Monge

M Place Monge. Open Wed & Fri 7am–2.30pm, Sun 7am–3pm.

Charming open-air market brimming with lovely meats, fish, cheeses, salads, and more. It has a lovely village atmosphere. Some stalls serve cooked food so you could have lunch here after your market tour. Early birds could enjoy a pain au chocolat on nearby rue Mouffetard.

Marché aux Puces d'Aligre

M Ledru-Rollin. Place de l'Aligre. Open Tue–Sun 7.30am–1.30pm.

A flea market full of vintage fashions and bric-a-brac. Marché Beauvau next door is a covered market full of gourmet food stands selling everything from spices and cheese to local beers and game.

Marché aux Puces

M Poret-de-Clignancourt. Open Sat 9am–6pm, Sun 10am–6pm, Mon 11am–5pm (subject to change). The most famous market in Paris selling anything from old uniforms to antiques. Over 150,000 eager bargain hunters come here each weekend to browse the 2,500 or so stalls, so get there early to avoid the afternoon crowds. Beware of pickpockets and keep valuables hidden.

MARKETS

133

RESTAURANTS

Here's a selection of restaurants, some typically Parisian in style, serving French or international cuisine. They are listed by price range and by district (for a list of the areas corresponding to each *arrondissement see p 154*). Bistros are generally small restaurants serving relatively simple meals in modest surroundings, while brasseries are a little more upscale; a *salon de thé* is a tea room.

Luxury	€€€€ over 60€	*Moderate*	€€ 20–35€
Expensive	€€€ 35–60€	*Inexpensive*	€ under 20€

1st and 2nd arr

L'Arbre à Cannelle
€ **Salon de thé**
Ⓜ *Grands Boulevards. 57 passage des Panoramas. 01 45 08 55 87. Closed eves, Sun, public holidays, and 2 weeks in Aug, Dec 25–1 Jan.*
A former *chocolaterie* with 19C woodwork and a tea room. If you are tempted by quiches, pies, and salads, ask for a table in the room with the ornamental ceiling.

Café de l'Époque
€€ **Bistro**
Ⓜ *Palais-Royal-Musée-du-Louvre. 2 rue du Bouloi, Galerie Véro-Dodat. 01 42 33 40 70.*
This restaurant at the entrance to the Véro-Dodat Gallery, with authentic bistro decor. Traditional fare: salads, terrines, *foie gras, andouillette* and homemade pastries.

Le Gallopin
€€ **Brasserie**
Ⓜ *Bourse. 40 rue N.-D.-des-Victoires. 01 42 36 45 38. www.brasseriegallopin.com.*
At this impressive, restored Paris brasserie—note the mahogany bar—the meals are served by staff in the traditional white aprons of French waiters, as befits the surroundings.

À La Grille Montorgueil
€€ **Bistro**
Ⓜ *Les Halles. 50 rue Montorgueil. 01 42 33 21 21. www.lagrille montorgueil.fr.*
In what was formerly a butcher's shop, this restaurant is now home to an attractive 1920s-style bistro. There is a superb bar at the entrance and a vaulted cellar. Typical bistro fare.

Café Marly
€€€ **Brasserie**
Ⓜ *Palais-Royal-Musée-du-Louvre. 93 rue de Rivoli . 01 49 26 06 60.*
Tucked under the Louvre's arcades, this hip restaurant serves contemporary cuisine. In summer be sure to have a drink out on the terrace—it's one of Paris's prettiest. Serves until 1am.

Café Ruc
€€€ **Café-restaurant**
Ⓜ *Palais-Royal-Musée-du-Louvre. 159 rue St-Honoré. 01 42 60 97 54. Reservations recommended.*
With its neo-Baroque style, Café Ruc's atmosphere is warm and welcoming. Its eclectic menu of modern cuisine makes it crowded in the fashion-show season.

MUST EAT

Le Grand Colbert

€€€ **Brasserie**

M *Bourse. 2 rue Vivienne. 01 42 86 87 88. www.legrandcolbert.com. Open daily midday–1am.*

Worthy of a film set, decorated with mosaics and murals, and a vast bar, this 19C brasserie is probably frequented more for the setting than the food. Fixed-price menu. Serves until 1am.

Café Drouant

€€€€ **Restaurant**

M *Quatre-Septembre. 16–18 place Gaillon. 01 42 65 15 16. www.drouant.com. Closed Aug.*

A Parisian institution, but for those who'd rather not risk bankruptcy, try the "Café Drouant" menu served in a more sober dining room.

Le Grand Vefour

€€€€ **Restaurant**

M *Palais-Royal-Musée-du-Louvre. 17 rue de Beaujolais. 01 42 96 56 27. www.grand-vefour.com. Closed Sat-Sun, Dec 23–25, and Jan 1.*

Beneath the arches of the Palais-Royal, this former 18C café is luxuriously decorated. Indulge in the famous *ravioles de foie gras*.

3rd and 4th arr

L'Apparemment

€ **Café-restaurant**

M *St-Sébastien-Froissart. 18 rue des Coutures, St-Gervais. 01 48 87 12 22. Closed Sat lunch. Reservations requested eves.*

An appealingly homey feel, decorated with an array of paintings and furniture. Fine selection of salads at lunchtime; cocktails and cold meals in the evening. Sunday brunch.

Chez Janou

€ **Brasserie**

M *Chemin-Vert. 2 rue Roger-Verlomme. 01 42 72 28 41. www.chezjanou.com.*

This charming 1900s bistro with original decor features a superb ceramic-covered wall. Good lunch specials and Provençal-style dishes.

Ambassade d'Auvergne

€€ **Restaurant**

M *Rambuteau. 22 rue du Grenier-St-Lazare. 01 42 72 31 22. www.ambassade-auvergne.com.*

The rustic ground-floor dining room will transport you to rural France. Hams and sausages hang above the large communal table. Perfect for fans of hearty Auvergne cuisine.

Bofinger

€€ **Brasserie**

M *Bastille. 5 rue de la Bastille. 01 42 72 87 82. www.bofinger paris.com.*

Founded in 1864, this Parisian landmark with its *belle époque* decor has fed some of the most famous politicians, writers, artists and musicians of the 20C. The brasserie, with its handsome glass roof, is as crowded today. Reservations recommended. Serves until 1am.

Chez Jenny

€€ **Brasserie**

M *République. 39 blvd du Temple. 01 44 54 39 00. www.chez-jenny.com.*

An Alsatian restaurant founded in 1932 by a craftsman and decorated with marquetry and sculptures (upper floor rooms). Brasserie-style cuisine.

Au Bourguignon du Marais
€€€ **Restaurant**
Ⓜ *Saint-Paul. 52 rue François-Miron. 01 48 87 15 40. Closed Mon, Sun, public holidays, and Jul 19 –Aug 28.*
A restaurant and wine merchant's showcasing Burgundy wines in a contemporary setting. Try the parsleyed house ham or the *Boeuf Bourguignon*.

L'Enoteca
€€€ **Restaurant**
Ⓜ *Sully-Morland. 25 rue Charles-V. 01 42 78 91 44. Closed 1 week in Aug. Reservations recommended.*
Creative Italian cuisine and wine in a charming 17C house with old beams, ocher-colored walls and hand-blown Murano lamps.

5th and 6th arr

Le Machon d'Henri
€ **Bistro**
Ⓜ *Mabillon. 8 rue Guisarde. 01 43 29 08 70.*
Often full at lunch, enjoy tasty little dishes of Lyonnais inspiration in a decor of exposed beams and painted stones. Lively atmosphere.

Au Piano Muet
€ **Restaurant**
Ⓜ *Place Monge. 48 rue Mouffetard. 01 43 31 45 15. Closed lunch except Sat–Sun.*
Perfect for warming winter food, with dishes such as raclettes and fondues, in a convivial atmosphere.

Bouillon Racine
€€ **Brasserie**
Ⓜ *Odéon. 3 rue Racine. 01 44 32 15 60. www.bouillon-racine.com.*
A former workers' canteen with a listed Art Nouveau decor serving typical French brasserie fare. Attentive service and a large selection of Belgian beers.

Brasserie Lipp
€€ **Brasserie**
Ⓜ *St-Germain-des-Près. 151 blvd St Germain. 01 45 48 53 91. Open 9am–1am.*
Waiters in waistcoats, delightful decor, and appealing ambience combine with a memorable menu to make this a good choice.

Mirama
€€ **Restaurant**
Ⓜ *St-Michel. 17 rue St-Jacques. 01 43 54 71 77.*
This Chinese restaurant is popular with tourists and locals. It serves generous helpings of well-prepared food at reasonable prices.

Le Perraudin
€€ **Bistro**
Ⓜ *Luxembourg. 157 rue St-Jacques. 01 46 33 15 75. www.restaurant-perraudin.com. Closed Sun and Aug.*
Straight out of a scene from a Maigret detective novel, with its checkered tablecloths, bar, and old mirrors. Appetizing bistro cuisine and *Tarte Tatin* for those with a sweet tooth. No reservations.

Le Petit Zinc
€€ **Restaurant**
Ⓜ *St-Germain-des-Près. 11 rue St Benoit. 01 42 86 61 00. www.petit-zinc.com. Open noon–2pm.*
If you feel like enjoying sea bass in a clay crust or a shoulder of lamb with garlic, head to this Art Nouveau gem. Enjoy eating on the terrace in the summer.

Le Petit Zinc

© Raoul Dobremel / Le Petit Zinc

Le Buisson Ardent
€€€ **Bistro**
Ⓜ *Jussieu. 01 43 54 93 02.*
www.lebuissonardent.fr.
25 rue Jussieu. Closed Aug.
With frescoes from 1923, this local-style bistro is always crowded. Relaxed, friendly atmosphere and good food.

La Ferrandaise
€€€ **Restaurant**
Ⓜ *Luxembourg. 8 rue de Vaugirard. 01 43 26 36 36. www.laferrandaise. com. Closed lunch Mon, and Sat, Sun and 3 weeks in Aug.*
Fresh, seasonal fare specializing in beef from the Puy-de-Dôme region of central France. A large selection of natural wines, and creative desserts. The cozy dining room has a rustic feel.

Le Reminet
€€€ **Restaurant**
Ⓜ *Maubert-Mutualité. 3 rue des Grands-Degrés. 01 44 07 04 24. www.lereminet.com. Closed 2 weeks in Feb, 3 weeks in Aug.*
Tasty cuisine, a fixed-price lunch menu, an affordable weekday

dinner menu, and a tempting wine list—what more could you ask?

Terroir Parisien
€€€ **Restaurant**
Ⓜ *Maubert-Mutualité. 20 rue Saint-Victoir. 01 44 31 54 54. www.yannick-alleno.com/carnet/ terroir-parisien.*
Chef Yannick Alleno uses the best local ingredients from the Paris region to breathe new life into French classics. The contemporary dining room in the Art Deco Maison de la Mutualité is stylish yet laid back. Seating at the bar also available.

Le Procope
Founded in 1686, this is the oldest cafe in Paris and serves an excellent *coq au vin ivre de Juliénas*. You will follow in the footsteps of Voltaire and Benjamin Franklin if you dine here. *(€€)* Ⓜ *Odéon. 3 rue de l'Ancienne Comedie. 01 40 46 79 00. www.procope.com. Open 11.45am–1am.*

RESTAURANTS

7th and 8th arr

Bar à Vin Nicolas
€ **Restaurant**
Ⓜ *Madeleine. 31 place de la Madeleine. 01 42 68 00 16. www.nicolas.com. Open Mon–Sat 9.30am–8pm.*
Nicolas wine stores are a familiar Parisian sight, but this one also has a restaurant where you can enjoy a glass of wine and a snack of salad, quiche, charcuterie, and cheese.

Chez Françoise
€€ **Brasserie**
Ⓜ *Invalides. Aerogare des Invalides. 01 47 05 49 03. www.chezfrancoise.com.*
Founded in 1949, this upscale brasserie has been given a facelift while still respecting its vintage style. Popular with the government representatives from the National Assembly next door.

Le P'tit Troquet
€€ **Bistro**
Ⓜ *École Militaire. 28 rue de l'Exposition. 01 47 05 80 39. Closed Sat & Mon lunch, Sun, and 2 weeks in Jan, 3 weeks in Aug. Reservations requested.*
Secondhand treasure hunters will like the bottles, mirrors, and other odds-and-bobs decorating the dining room. Market-fresh dishes that are popular with the locals.

Ribe
€€ **Restaurant**
Ⓜ *Champ-de-Mars–Tour-Eiffel. 15 ave de Suffren. 01 45 66 53 79.*
Parisians and tourists alike appreciate the reasonable prices as well as the traditional French dishes: onion soup, terrines, and steak in pepper sauce.

Le Vauban
€€ **Brasserie**
Ⓜ *St-François-Xavier. 7 place Vauban. 01 47 05 52 67.*
Try for a seat with a view of the Invalides on the popular terrace of this brasserie or else in the stylish dining room featuring trompe l'œil marble work.

58 Tour Eiffel
€€€ **Restaurant**
Ⓜ *La Tour Maubourg. Level 1, Eiffel Tower. 01 76 64 14 64. www.restaurants-toureiffel.com.*
Located in the Eiffel Tower itself, enjoy lunch (served in a picnic basket) or dinner while gazing out over an unforgettable view of Paris. Good French cuisine. Reserve well in advance for dinner, preferably several weeks before your trip.

9th and 10th arr

Hôtel du Nord
€ **Café-restaurant**
Ⓜ *Jacques-Bonsergent 102 quai de Jemmapes. 01 40 40 78 78. www.hoteldunord.org. Closed Sun 2 weeks in Aug.*
Immortalized in the classic film *Hôtel du Nord*, it still has a retro feel and serves classic cuisine for a young, trendy crowd. Reservations are recommended in the evenings. It's also possible to just have wine at the bar.

Brasserie Flo
€€ **Brasserie**
Ⓜ *Château-d'Eau. 7 cour des Petites-Écuries. 01 47 70 13 59. www.floparis.com.*
The old paintings and stained-glass windows of this turn-of-the-century brasserie create a

Hôtel du Nord

© Y. Kanazawa / MICHELIN

picturesque setting for the appetizing cuisine. Serves until as late as 1.30am.

Chez Marie-Louise
€€ **Bistro**
M *Goncourt. 11 rue Marie-et-Louise. 01 53 19 02 04. www.chezmarielouise.com. Closed weekends.*
A popular neo-bistro a few steps from the Canal Saint-Martin with retro decor and French classics written on the chalk board, such as rabbit terrine, roasted duck breast, vanilla millefeuille. Be sure to reserve a few days in advance.

Paprika
€€ **Restaurant**
M *Anvers. 28 ave Trudaine. 01 44 63 02 91. www.le-paprika.com. Closed Jan 1, Dec 24–25.*
On the same spot as the Âne Rouge, where socialist radicals rallied in the early 20C, this is now a Hungarian restaurant. Try the Hungarian wines and dishes including cold meats.

Au Petit Riche
€€ **Restaurant**
M *Le Peletier. 25 rue Le Peletier. 01 47 70 68 68. www.restaurant-aupetitriche.com.*
Since 1858, bankers and stockbrokers have convened in the comfort of this restaurant. Excellent selection of Loire wines. Serves until 12.15pm and attracts the post-theater crowd.

Le Barramundi
€€€ **Restaurant**
M *Richelieu-Drouot. 3 rue Taitbout. 01 47 70 21 21. www.barramundi.fr. Closed Sat lunch, Sun, and 10 days in Aug.*
"World" music plays in the bar-lounge, while downstairs the spacious restaurant is popular with the business lunch bunch. Mediterranean cuisine with a tang.

Le Pantruche
€€€ **Bistro**
M *Pigalle. 3 rue Victor Massé. 01 48 78 55 60. www.lepantruche.com. Closed weekends, and 3 weeks in Aug.*
"Pantruche" is slang for the working

class Parisians who frequented Pigalle in the 1940s. Today this convivial gourmet bistro creates a warm atmosphere for family gatherings over hearty French classics. Dishes include inventive takes on foie gras terrine, oyster tartare, suckling pig, scallops, black truffle risotto, line-caught cod, Grand Marnier soufflet.

11th and 12th arr

Chez l'Artiste
€ **Restaurant**
Ⓜ *Philippe-Auguste. 153 rue de la Roquette. 01 43 79 96 19. www.restaurant-lartiste.fr.*
A pretty Italian restaurant, modern and cozy, with a fine selection of pastas and salads. The superb terrace under the trees is perfect for a summer meal or afternoon *aperitif*.

Le Grand Bleu
€ **Restaurant**
Ⓜ *Bastille. 11 blvd de la Bastille, Arsenal yacht harbor. 01 43 45 19 99.*
Seated at the terrace overlooking the capital's marina and garden, you're a stone's throw from the Bastille. Meals are served on the veranda when the sun is playing hard to get. Fish and seafood specialties.

Bistrot Les Sans Culottes
€€ **Bistro**
Ⓜ *Bastille. 27 rue de Lappe. 01 48 05 42 92. www.bistrotles sansculottes.com.*
Before venturing into the nocturnal throng of the rue de Lappe, stop off here and check out the turn-of-the-century appeal of this bistro.

Jean-Pierre Frelet
€€ **Restaurant**
Ⓜ *Montgallet. 25 rue Montgallet. 01 43 43 76 65. Closed Sat lunch, Sun, and Feb school vacations, Aug.*
It's easy to miss the narrow façade of this restaurant, but don't as the food is too good. The owner-chef worked for years in France's best restaurants before opening his own.

Blue Elephant
€€€ **Restaurant**
Ⓜ *Bastille, Voltaire. 43 rue de la Roquette. 01 47 00 42 00. www.blueelephant.com. Closed Sat lunch.*
A little corner of Thailand in the shadow of the Bastille. Decor of green plants and wicker furniture. It's like stepping into another world rich with a thousand flavors. Service until midnight.

Maison Chardenoux
€€€ **Bistro**
Ⓜ *Charonne. 1 rue Jules-Vallès. 01 43 71 49 52. www.restaurant lechardenoux.com.*
A real live Parisian bistro! With its authentic decor from 1904, this little restaurant is as inviting as can be. A bit of a squeeze in the narrow dining room but delicious, revitalizing cuisine.

Le Train Bleu
€€€€ **Brasserie**
Ⓜ *Gare de Lyon. At the Gare de Lyon (1st floor). 01 43 43 09 06. www.le-train-bleu.com.*
A must! This opulent brasserie with its luxurious frescoes and moldings covered in gold-leaf truly belongs to Parisian historic heritage. Originally designed for weary

rail travelers, it's now a gourmet restaurant. The English-style bar is a pleasant place for afternoon tea and light meals.

13th, 14th, 15th arr

Chez Gladines
€ **Restaurant**
Ⓜ *Corvisart. 30 rue des Cinq-Diamants. 01 45 80 70 10. Closed 3 weeks in Aug.*
This country-style Basque restaurant in the Butte-aux-Cailles is always full. Big salads with potatoes and bacon served in a rustic decor.

L'Infinithé
€ **Salon de thé**
Ⓜ *Convention. 8 rue Desnouettes. 01 40 43 14 23. www.infinithe.com. Closed eves, Mon, Sun except the 1st Sun of each month. Reservations recommended.*
This tiny *salon de thé* does a fine job of reviving the 1930s. Wooden dressers, small tables, and embroidered tablecloths contribute to the atmosphere. Delicious pastries.

Le Beau Violet
€€ **Restaurant**
Ⓜ *Commerce. 92 rue des Entrepreneurs. 01 45 78 93 44. Closed Sun and Aug. Reservations required .*
The perfect place for a culinary trip to Corsica. The dishes, simmered in the hearth and served in copper ovenware, are heavenly.

Au Moulin Vert
€€ **Restaurant**
Ⓜ *Alésia. 34 bis rue des Plantes. 01 45 39 31 31. www.aumoulin vert.com.*
Opened in 1905, with house plants on the veranda and a backdrop of trees, a green haven where the classic fare is excellent value. Regular live jazz nights.

Nouveau Village Tao-Tao
€€ **Restaurant**
Ⓜ *Nationale. 159 blvd Vincent-Auriol. 01 45 86 40 08.*
Just a few strides from Chinatown, Thai dishes are also served in the typically orientalist decor; the fixed-price lunch menus are particularly good value.

La Régalade
€€ **Bistro**
Ⓜ *Alésia. 49 avenue J.-Moulin. 01 45 45 68 58. Closed Mon, Sun, and Aug. Reservations required.*
A typical Parisian bistro offering first-rate meals in the crowded dining room. Regional cuisine and tastes based on the daily market offerings. Two other locations now open in the 1st and 9th districts.

♿ La Coupole
€€€ **Brasserie**
Ⓜ *Vavin. 102 blvd du Montparnasse. 01 43 20 14 20. www.lacoupoleparis.com.*
A temple of Parisian nightlife that needs no introduction. A famous nightclub in the early 20C, this 1920s brasserie has retained its splendid original decor, superb bar, and long bay windows. It continues to cater to night owls in a lively atmosphere until 1am. *See Nightlife.*

RESTAURANTS

Carette

€ **Salon de thé**

Ⓜ *Trocadéro. 4 place du Trocadéro. 01 47 27 98 85. www.carette-paris.com.*

Founded in 1927, this pretty pink tea room with the vast covered terrace is a classic. Tea and pastries served in dainty china cups. The *macarons* are a must, made with the original Carette recipe.

Café d'Angel

€€ **Bistro**

Ⓜ *Ternes. 16 rue Brey. 01 47 54 03 33. Closed Sat–Sun, and Aug, Christmas–New Year.*

A medium-sized establishment not from the Arc de Triomphe, where the latest cuisine is served amid slightly old-fashioned decor. Leatherette benches, old tiles, and a slate menu set the tone. Quite reasonably priced at lunchtime.

La Gare

€€ **Restaurant**

Ⓜ *La Muette. 19 Chaussée de la Muette. 01 42 15 15 31. www.restaurantlagare.com.*

Dinner on the platform or a quick lunch in the waiting room: you're dining in the old Passy-La Muette train station. Built in 1854, it now houses a restaurant. Lively cuisine and terrace in summer. Brunch on Sundays with fun for children. Serves until midnight.

Grain d'orge

€€ **Restaurant**

Ⓜ *Charles-de-Gaulle-Étoile. 15 rue de l'Arc-de-Triomphe. 01 47 64 33 47. www.le-graindorge.fr. Closed Sat lunch, Sun.*

Red velvet wall seats, large mirrors and handsome bar are characteristic of the Art Deco style. Wine list enhanced by a choice of beers.

Caves Petrissans

€€€ **Bistro**

Ⓜ *Pereire, Ternes. 30 bis ave Niel. 01 42 27 5203. www.caves-petrissans.fr. Closed Sat–Sun and end Jul–early Aug.*

Over 100 years old and a Parisian institution. The convivial atmosphere, refreshing cuisine, and fine wine cellar contribute to its success.

Le Pré Catelan

€€€€ **Restaurant**

Route de Suresnes in Bois de Boulogne – from Porte Maillot take the Allée de Longchamp, then the Allée de la Reine. 01 44 14 41 14. www.precatelanparis.com. Closed Mon, Sun, and 2 weeks in Feb, 3 weeks in Aug, 1 week around Nov 1.

In the Bois de Boulogne on the edge of the enchanting Pré-Catelan garden, the luxurious interior, garden, and beautiful summer terrace beguile the Paris elite who continue to flock here to enjoy the exceptional (Michelin-starred) cuisine.

Le Vieux Chalet

€ **Bistro**

Ⓜ *Abbesses, Anvers. 14 bis rue Norvins. 01 46 06 21 44. Closed Sat, Sun eve, Mon, and Dec–Mar.*

A hundred-year-old countrified inn with a lovely terrace-garden far from the madding crowd, though not far from the place du Tertre, frequented by Apollinaire and Picasso in their day. Unpretentious home-style cooking.

Bistro Chantefable

€€ **Bistro**

Ⓜ *Gambetta. 93 ave Gambetta. 01 46 36 81 76. www.chantefable.fr. Closed Dec 24–25.*

After paying your respects at the Père-Lachaise cemetery, come and join the living in this bistro behind the town hall. The selection of wines, seafood, and convivial ambience amid charming retro decor are a hit with the locals.

L'Été en Pente Douce

€€ **Restaurant-salon de thé**

Ⓜ *Anvers. 23 rue Muller. 01 42 64 02 67. www.parisresto.com. Closed Dec 25, Jan 1.*

Down a side street a few steps from Sacré-Cœur, take a seat on the terrace of this former baker's shop and choose from salads, pastas, mixed platters, and pastries, opposite a pretty public garden.

L'Hermès

€€ **Restaurant**

Ⓜ *Pyrénées. 23 rue Mélingue. 01 42 39 94 70. Closed Sun, Mon, Wed lunch, and Easter, Aug.*

Finding the discreet blue façade of this small restaurant near the Buttes-Chaumont takes some doing, but it's worth the effort. The lunch menu is a bargain.

La Mère Catherine

€€ **Bistro**

Ⓜ *Abbesses. 6 place du Tertre. 01 46 06 32 69. www.lamerecatherine.com.*

In the heart of Montmartre, this 17C restaurant became famous after Danton and his followers came here. A rustic interior and a terrace that is busy when the sun shines.

Rughetta

€€ **Restaurant**

Ⓜ *Blanche. 41 rue Lepic. 01 42 23 41 70. Closed Christmas, New Year. Reservations recommended.*

A delightful little Italian restaurant. The closely set tables are besieged as the chef skillfully whips up dishes from his native land.

Chatomat

€€€ **Bistro**

Ⓜ *Ménilmontant. 6 rue Victor Letalle. 01 47 97 25 77. Open dinner Tue–Sat and first Sun of the month. Closed Christmas, New Year. Reservations recommended.*

A modern bistro well-hidden from the beaten path with exposed stone walls and just a few tables for those in the know. The seasonal dishes are inventive, fresh, and precise, making the most of each ingredient without overdoing it.

RESTAURANTS

HOTELS

Paris offers a wide range of accommodation at all price levels. The hotels selected here cover a variety of locations, facilities, and prices (including tents!). We have grouped them first into four price categories, and then alphabetically within each category. Rooms are rented by the night and the prices shown reflect the average cost for a standard double room occupied by two people in high season—but do check the websites for seasonal variations and special offers. Breakfast is usually extra, so we show the cost here. It is important to book ahead—Parisian hotels can get very busy, in particular during the high season (Easter to October and Christmas/New Year). August is generally a quieter month as many Parisians are on vacation then—but other tourists will be in town! Be aware that many hotels expect you to reconfirm if you plan to arrive after 5pm or 6pm. Failure to do so could result in losing your reservation, so do let them know your arrival time.

| *Luxury* | €€€€ | **over €150** | *Moderate* | €€ | **€80–€90** |
| *Expensive* | €€€ | **€90–€130** | *Budget* | € | **€70** |

Camping Le Bois de Boulogne
€   **510 sites**
Allée du Bord-de-l'Eau (between the Suresnes Bridge and the Puteaux Bridge). 01 45 24 30 00. www.campingparis.fr. Reservations recommended. Food service.

Located in the Bois de Boulogne, and predictably noisy, but the prices are hard to beat. Sites closest to the Seine are the quietest. Prices for a tent (no car) start at 17.10€. In summer there's a shuttle service to and from the Porte-Maillot Métro station every 15 minutes. Mobile home rentals available.

Hôtel Andréa Rivoli
€   **32 rooms**
Ⓜ *Hôtel-de-Ville. 3 rue St-Bon. 01 42 78 43 93. www.hotelandrea rivoli.fr. Breakfast 9€.*

You won't regret having chosen this renovated, well located, central hotel. Modern decor and air conditioning throughout.

Hôtel Chopin
€   **36 rooms**
Ⓜ *Richelieu-Drouot. 10 blvd Montmartre, 46 passage Jouffroy. 01 47 70 58 10. www.hotelchopin.fr. Breakfast 8€.*

Located in a covered passage dating from 1846, this pleasant hotel is surprisingly quiet given the lively neighborhood. Colorful rooms. Book well ahead.

Hôtel Libertel Gare de l'Est Français
€   **70 rooms**
Ⓜ *Gare-de-l'Est. 13 rue du 8-Mai-1945. 01 40 35 94 14. www.hotelfrancais.com. Breakfast 11€.*

Opposite the busy Gare de l'Est, this hotel offers good value rooms that are clean, well-equipped, soundproofed and air-conditioned. Family rooms available.

MUST STAY

Hôtel Lilas-Gambetta
€   **34 rooms**
Ⓜ *Porte-des-Lilas. 223 av. Gambetta. 01 40 31 85 60. www.lilas-gambetta.com. Breakfast 9.50€.*
The 1925 façade of brick and cut stone conceals a contemporary interior and furniture from the 1970s and 80s that will charm fans of the era. The most peaceful rooms give onto a small courtyard where breakfast is served in summer.

Hôtel de Paris
€   **30 rooms**
Ⓜ *Place-de-Clichy or La Fourche. 17 rue Biot. 01 42 94 02 50. www.hoteldeparis-montmartre.com.*
This refurbished hotel is in a great location near place de Clichy—just below Montmartre with all its attractions, and near a major shopping area. The small rooms all come with good bathrooms. Breakfasts are served on the patio in summer.

Hôtel Stella
€   **24 rooms**
Ⓜ *Odéon. 41 rue Monsieur le Prince. 01 40 51 00 25. http://stella-hotel.voila.net.*
Traditional Parisian romantic old-world charm means no elevator and no TV, but exposed wooden beams, tiled floors, and a wonky staircase. Pick your room online.

Hôtel Tiquetonne
€   **47 rooms**
Ⓜ *Étienne-Marcel. 6 rue Tiquetonne. 01 42 36 94 58. www.hoteltiquetonne.fr. Breakfast 8€.*
This modest family hotel is situated near the shopping center of Les Halles and the fashionable Rue Montorgueil. The bright rooms, with their old-fashioned charm, are quite well kept and, above all, very inexpensive. Rooms have free wifi.

Hôtel de Venise
€   **28 rooms**
Ⓜ *Reuilly-Diderot. 4 rue Chaligny. 01 43 43 63 45. www.hotelde venise.fr. Breakfast 8.50€.*
This family-run establishment is located near the original Viaduc des Arts and offers practical rooms with bath and wifi. Warm welcome.

Résidence du Palais
€   **24 rooms**
Ⓜ *Odéon. 78 rue d'Assas. 01 43 26 79 32. www.hotelresidence dupalais.com. Breakfast 12€.*
Overlooking the Luxembourg Gardens, this family-run residence has basic but spacious rooms, with quadruples and suites for families. Long stays at reduced rates.

Balladins la Villette Hôtel
€€   **40 rooms**
Ⓜ *Crimée. 219 rue de Crimée. 01 40 38 91 00. www.balladins.com. Breakfast 9€.*
Those visiting La Villette and its many attractions will appreciate the proximity of this hotel. Pleasant, renovated rooms and agreeable breakfast salon, free wifi.

Comfort Hôtel Place du Tertre
€€   **50 rooms**
Ⓜ *Abbesses or Blanche. 16 rue Tholozé. 01 42 55 05 06. www.comfort-placedutertre.com. Breakfast 10€.*
Great location between the Moulin de la Galette and the Rue des Abbesses and yet very peaceful. Refurbished, practical rooms decorated in pale neutrals and contemporary furnishngs.

Grand Hôtel des Balcons
€€   **50 rooms**
Ⓜ *Odéon. 3 rue Casimir-Delavigne. 01 46 34 78 50. www.hotelgrands balcons.com. Breakfast 15€.*
A charming, Art Nouveau style hotel with contemporary decor in the rooms and small balconies overlooking the street. Reasonable prices for the neighborhood.

Ermitage Hôtel
€€   **12 rooms**
Ⓜ *Lamarck-Caulaincourt. 24 rue Lamarck. 01 42 64 79 22. www.ermitagesacrecoeur.fr.*
Originally built by a wealthy man for his mistress, this 19C townhouse now boasts personalzied rooms, four overlooking the rooftops, others with a terrace onto the garden. Breakfast included.

Hôtel de l'Avre
€€   **26 rooms**
Ⓜ *La Motte-Picquet-Grenelle. 21 rue de l'Avre. 01 45 75 31 03. www.hotel delavre.com. Breakfast 10.50€.*
Bright colors reminiscent of Provence and a verdant garden in which to enjoy breakfast await. Tasteful, quiet bedrooms, and a simple yet cozy ambience.

Hôtel Campanile
€€   **161 rooms**
Ⓜ *Chemin-Vert. 9 rue du Chemin-Vert. 01 43 38 58 08. www.campanile.com. Breakfast 9.90€.*
A modern chain hotel between Bastille and République. All rooms have air conditioning and free wifi, some have a terrace and in fine weather, breakfast is served in the tiny garden.

Hôtel Caravelle
€€   **38 rooms**
Ⓜ *Bonne-Nouvelle or Poissonnière. 41 rue des Petites Écuries. 01 45 23 08 22. www.caravelle-paris-hotel.com. Breakfast 8€.*
Located in a quiet area with clean, smallish, colorful bedrooms. Not far from Gare de l'Est and Gare du Nord.

Hôtel Delambre
€€   **30 rooms**
Ⓜ *Vavin or Edgar-Quinet. 35 rue Delambre. 01 43 20 66 31. www.delambre-paris-hotel.com. Breakfast 12€.*
This fully refurbished boutique hotel a few minutes from Montparnasse has bright, functional rooms, and a warm welcome. Good prices.

Hôtel Le 20 Prieuré
€€   **32 rooms**
Ⓜ *Oberkampf. 20 rue du Grand-Prieuré. 01 47 00 74 14. www.hotel20prieure.com. Breakfast 15€.*
Near the Marais and Place des Vosges, this completely renovated boutique hotel has contemporary decor with Parisian monuments screened onto the walls and air conditioning.

Hôtel Jeanne d'Arc
€€   **36 rooms**
Ⓜ *Saint-Paul or Bastille. 3 rue de Jarente. 01 48 87 62 11. www.hoteljeannedarc.com. Breakfast 8€.*
This unpretentious hotel built in the 17C has old-fashioned, eclectic decor and rooftop views over the Marais from the 6th floor. It offers comfort at reasonable prices, so be sure to book ahead.

MUST STAY

Hôtel Malar
€€ **22 rooms**
Ⓜ École-Militaire or La Tour-Maubourg. 29 rue Malar. 01 45 51 38 46. www.hotelmalar.com. Breakfast 11€.
Good location for the Eiffel Tower. The eclectic rooms have pretty bathrooms and summer breakfasts are served in the small inner courtyard.

Hôtel de Nesle
€€ **20 rooms**
Ⓜ Odéon. 7 rue de Nesle. 01 43 54 62 41. www.hotelde nesleparis.com.
A quirky hotel in the center of the Latin Quarter. Each room is decorated with a different theme, and a small courtyard garden is perfect for lounging in summer. Reservations by phone only.

Hôtel New Orient
€€ **30 rooms**
Ⓜ Europe or Villiers. 16 rue de Constantinople. 01 45 22 21 64. www.hotel-paris-orient.com. Breakfast 13€.
This hotel's inviting façade is in perfect keeping with the smart interior. The wooden staircase and immaculate rooms complement the warm, hospitable ambience. Air conditioning and free wifi.

Hôtel du Nord et de l'Est
€€ **45 rooms**
Ⓜ Oberkampf. 49 rue de Malte. 01 47 00 71 70. www.parishotel nordest.com. Breakfast 10€.
A small unassuming hotel in a quiet street near République. Run by the same family since 1929, who offer a cheerful welcome that makes you feel at home instantly. Wifi provided.

Hôtel Paris-Gambetta
€€ **32 rooms**
Ⓜ Gambetta. 12 av. du Père-Lachaise. 01 47 97 76 57. www.hotelparisgambetta.com. Breakfast 10€.
This appealing hotel is located close to the Père-Lachaise cemetery, resting-place of so many celebrities. The hotel provides a tranquil stopover in a street that is shielded from the urban fracas all around. The well-soundproofed rooms are furnished in the style of the 1980s.

Hôtel Résidence Vert Galant
€€ **15 rooms**
Ⓜ Les Gobelins. 43 rue Croulebarbe. 01 44 08 83 50. www.vertgalant.com. Breakfast 10€.
By a large park on a quiet street, a pleasant hotel boasting a private garden, some rooms with kitchenettes, its own Basque restaurant (€€; popular with locals), and wifi.

Hôtel Romance Malesherbes
€€ **21 rooms**
Ⓜ Villiers or Malesherbes. 129 rue Cardinet. 01 44 15 85 00. Breakfast 11€.
This small boutique hotel near the Batignolle Gardens has rooms decorated in a contemporary, romantic theme with chic Parisian wall coverings. Some rooms have kitchenettes.

HOTELS

Hôtel de Roubaix

€€   **53 rooms**

Ⓜ *Réaumur-Sebastopol. 6 rue Greneta. 01 42 72 89 91. www.hotel-de-roubaix.com.*

An old-fashioned and inexpensive hotel close to the Centre Pompidou and Les Halles. Some rooms have pop-art decor. Tiled bathrooms with walk-in showers and breakfast included. Book ahead.

République Hôtel

€€   **40 rooms**

Ⓜ *République. 31 rue Albert-Thomas. 01 42 39 19 03. www.republiquehotel.com. Breakfast 8€.*

In a quiet street between Place de la République and the Saint-Martin Canal, this hotel offers simple comfort with fun pop-art touches and reasonable prices.

Résidence Les Gobelins

€€   **32 rooms**

Ⓜ *Les Gobelins. 9 rue des Gobelins. 01 47 07 26 90. www.hotelgobelins.com. Breakfast 9€.*

On a small paved road next to the Gobelins tapestry factory, this hotel has small, quiet, and colorful rooms, and a pretty, flower-decked patio near the breakfast room.

Résidence du Pré

€€   **40 rooms**

Ⓜ *Poissonnière. 15 rue Pierre-Sémard. 01 48 78 26 72. www. residence.leshotelsdupre.com. Breakfast 11€.*

Two minutes from the Gare du Nord, this modest establishment is well-maintained. Rooms are clean and functional and have free wifi.

Timhotel Tour Eiffel

€€   **39 rooms**

Ⓜ *Dupleix. 11 rue Juge. 01 45 78 29 29. www.timhotel.com. Breakfast € 11.50.*

Close to the Eiffel Tower and shopping areas, this hotel has comfortable, basic decor plus convenient Métro links to the center of Paris.

Grand Hôtel Français

€€€   **40 rooms**

Ⓜ *Nation. 223 blvd Voltaire. 01 43 71 27 57. www.grand-hotel-francais.fr. Breakfast 10€.*

In a good location a stone's throw from the Place de la Nation and the principal Métro and RER lines, this is a stylish hotel in a beautiful building. Wifi and soundproofing.

Grand Hôtel Lévêque

€€€   **50 rooms**

Ⓜ *École-Militaire. 29 rue Cler. 01 47 05 49 15. www.hotel-leveque.com. Breakfast 10€.*

A rare find, in a lively little street in the shadow of the École Militaire, offering, well-furnished, remodelled rooms in contemporary decor and affordable prices. Air-conditioning, wifi, and all day bar.

Hôtel du 7e Art

€€€   **23 rooms**

Ⓜ *Saint-Paul. 20 rue St-Paul. 01 44 54 85 00. 23. www.paris-hotel-7art.com. rooms. Breakfast 8€.*

The name says it all: the films of 1940–60 form the motif of this hotel. Ask for a room with exposed beams on the 3rd or 4th floor. Guest laundry room. The breakfast room has a rustic appeal.

MUST STAY

Hôtel du 7e Art

© photo ELIOPHOT – Aix en Provence / Hôtel du 7e Art

Hôtel d'Albion
€€€ **26 rooms**
Ⓜ *Miromesnil. 15 rue de Penthièvre. 01 42 65 84 15. www.hotelalbion.net. Breakfast 10€.*
Between the Champs-Élysées and La Madeleine, this hotel is quiet with spacious rooms (ask for courtyard room). Summer breakfasts served in a secret garden.

Hôtel Ambassade
€€€ **38 rooms**
Ⓜ *Boissière or Kléber. 79 rue Lauriston. 01 45 53 41 15. www.hotelambassade.com. Breakfast 14€.*
This renovated hotel in a residential neighborhood offers peace and quiet and easy access the Champs-Élysées. Rooms have Art Deco interiors, air-conditioning, and granite bathrooms.

Hôtel Daguerre
€€€ **30 rooms**
Ⓜ *Denfert-Rochereau. 94 rue Daguerre. 01 43 22 43 54. www.hotelmontparnasse daguerre.com. Breakfast 10€.*
Renovated hotel in lively Montparnasse district with reasonable prices and comfotable rooms with air conditioning.

Hôtel de L'Empereur
€€€ **38 rooms**
Ⓜ *École-Militaire or La Tour-Maubourg. 2 rue Chevert. 01 45 55 88 02. Breakfast 12€.*
Contemporary style with a touch of Empire influence in this renovated hotel located just opposite the Invalides—a tip of the hat to Napoleon, buried under the Dome.

Hôtel des Grandes Écoles
€€€ **51 rooms**
Ⓜ *Cardinal Lemoine. 75 rue du Cardinal Lemoine. 01 43 26 79 23. www.hotel-grandes-ecoles.com. Breakfast 9€.*
These three houses include a pretty garden that provides a welcome oasis. The main building has retained its somewhat old-fashioned charm, while the other two have been tastefully renovated.

Hôtel du Mont-Blanc
€€€ **42 rooms**

Ⓜ *St-Michel. 28 rue de la Huchette. 01 43 54 22 29. Breakfast 8€.*
Located in a little street lined with bars and restaurants, this hotel opposite the legendary Théâtre de la Huchette is perfect for those looking for a lively neighborhood. Functional rooms and reasonably priced for the capital.

Hôtel de la Place des Vosges
€€€ **16 rooms**

Ⓜ *Bastille. 12 rue de Birague. 01 42 72 60 46. www.hotelplace desvosges.com. Breakfast 8€.*
Here's a hotel with character. Built in the 17C, its reasonably sized rooms are simply furnished. A sophisticated stopover next to one of the most beautiful squares in Paris.

Hôtel Le Quartier Bercy Square
€€€ **57 rooms**

Ⓜ *Daumesnil or Dugommier. 33 blvd de Reuilly. 01 44 87 09 09. www.lequartierhotelbs.com rooms. Breakfast 10€.*
Despite being located right in the heart of Paris, this hotel provides a peaceful port in the city's storm. Most of the smallish but neat rooms look out onto the two inner courtyards. Breakfast is served outdoors in summer, and on the veranda in winter.

Hôtel Sacré Cœur
€€€ **49 rooms**

Ⓜ *Lamarck-Caulaincourt. 101 rue Caulaincourt. 01 42 62 02 02. www.hotelroma.fr Breakfast 11€.*
Two minutes from the Sacré-Cœur in one of Montmartre's livelier streets, this hotel provides accommodation in the heart of the artists' quarter. The brightly-coloured, functional rooms are soundproofed. Air conditioning on top floors only.

Hôtel St-Jacques
€€€ **36 rooms**

Ⓜ *Maubert-Mutualité. 35 rue des Écoles. 01 44 07 45 45. www.paris-hotel-stjacques.com. Breakfast 12€.*
This 19C Latin Quarter building retains original plaster moldings. The bedrooms are spacious, decorated with tasteful furniture and well soundproofed. Reasonably priced. Narrow, with good bathrooms.

Hôtel Saphir Grenelle
€€€ **32 rooms**

Ⓜ *La Motte-Picquet – Grenelle. 10 rue du Commerce. 01 45 75 12 23. www.saphirhotel.fr. Breakfast 10€.*
A minute's walk from the Eiffel Tower, this unpretentious hotel offers practical rooms, some overlooking the inner courtyard where breakfast is served in summer.

Queen's Hôtel
€€€ **17 rooms**

Ⓜ *Michel-Ange Auteuil. 4 rue Bastien-Lepage. 01 42 88 89 85. www.hotel-queens-hotel.com. Breakfast 10€.*
Tucked away in a quiet street, this small hotel run by an ex-journalist has an eclectic style. Each room is named after a contemporary artist whose works appear on the walls. Six rooms have a jacuzzi. Wifi.

Grand Hôtel St-Michel
€€€€   **46 rooms**

Ⓜ *Luxembourg. 19 rue Cujas. 01 46 33 33 02. www.hotel-saintmichel-paris.com. Breakfast 20€.*

Located near the Sorbonne university and the Luxembourg Gardens, this completely renovated boutique hotel has contemporary rooms with colors that pop and sleek bathrooms. Steam bath and fitness room, as well as afternoon tea services.

Hôtel Avia
€€€€   **40 rooms**

Ⓜ *Pasteur. 181 rue de Vaugirard. 01 43 06 43 80. www.saphirhotel.fr. Breakfast 8.50€.*

A modern hotel close to Montparnasse and the Porte de Versailles. Bedrooms are spacious, well equipped with bright fabrics.

Hôtel Banville
€€€€   **38 rooms**

Ⓜ *Porte-de-Champerret. 166 blvd Berthier. 01 42 67 70 16. www.hotelbanville.fr. Breakfast 20€.*

A chic, romantic hotel managing to combine classic and contemporary styles. All the rooms are delightful, from Amélie's Room, complete with terrace, to Marie's Apartment, with rooftop views over Paris. Live music on Thursday nights in the lounge.

Hôtel Bretonnerie
€€€   **22 rooms, 7 suites**

Ⓜ *Hôtel-de-Ville. 22 rue Ste-Croix-de-la-Bretonnerie. 01 48 87 77 63. www.bretonnerie.com. Breakfast 10€.*

Treat yourself to a sojourn in this private 17C mansion in the heart of the Marais. The peaceful environment, beamed ceilings, and old-fashioned fabrics, so appropriate to the Marias area, all add extra appeal.

Hôtel Gavarni
€€€   **25 rooms**

Ⓜ *Passy. 5 rue Gavarni. 01 45 24 52 82. www.gavarniparishotel.com. Breakfast 18€.*

Perfect for the shops in rue de Passy. Red brick façade but with green credentials (it's an eco hotel) and refurbished interior with elegant touches. Rooms compact and stylish. Friendly welcome.

Hôtel Istria
€€€   **26 rooms**

Ⓜ *Raspail. 29 rue Campagne Première. 01 43 20 91 82. www.hotel-istria-paris.com. Breakfast 12€.*

Man Ray stayed in this small hotel, popular with many artists of Montparnasse's golden era. Refurbished but it has still retained the charm of its colorful past.

Hôtel la Manufacture
€€€   **56 rooms**

Ⓜ *Place-d'Italie. 8 rue Philippe-de-Champagne. 01 45 35 45 25. www.hotel-la-manufacture.com. Breakfast 12€.*

Close to the Place d'Italie, a modern, chic hotel with bar, sound-proofing, and air conditioning. Five of the top floor rooms are larger and one has a view of the Eiffel Tower.

Hôtel Muguet
€€€ **48 rooms**

Ⓜ *École-Militaire or La Tour-Maubourg. 11 rue Chevert. 01 47 05 05 93. www.hotelparismuguet.com. Breakfast 12€.*

Small hotel set in a quiet side street between the École Militaire and the Invalides. The well-maintained rooms are spotless and air-conditioned. Free wifi.

Hôtel du Palais-Bourbon
€€€ **32 rooms**

Ⓜ *Varenne. 49 rue de Bourgogne. 01 44 11 30 70. www.bourbon-paris-hotel.com. Breakfast 8€.*

Built in 1730, this hotel near the Rodin museum and the Invalides is a pleasant surprise. The attractive rooms have parquet floors, wood furniture, and air conditioning. Single rooms are small though very good value, while the doubles are spacious.

Hôtel Britannique
€€€€ **39 rooms**

Ⓜ *Châtelet. 01 42 33 74 59. 20 av. Victoria. www.hotel-britannique.fr. Breakfast 18€.*

Located just behind Châtelet, and a short walk across a bridge to the Île de la Cité, this hotel is reminiscent of an Agatha Christie novel in style. It has pleasant rooms and provides ample breakfasts.

La Maison Favart
€€€€ **37 rooms**

Ⓜ *Richelieu-Drouot. 01 42 97 59 83. 5 rue Marivaux. www.lamaison favart.com. Breakfast 30€.*

Luxurious 18th-century style with a playful twist, this hotel opposite the Opéra-Comique in a lively area has a sauna, fitness center and relaxation pool.

Hôtel Pavillon de la Reine
€€€€ **31 rooms**

Ⓜ *Chemin-Vert. 28 pl. des Vosges. 01 40 29 19 19. www.pavillon-de-la-reine.com. Breakfast 34€.*

Set in a courtyard garden on the gem-like Place des Vosges, this is one the most beautiful hotels in the city. Secluded with refined decor, beautiful fabrics, and antique furniture. There is also a spa with fitness center.

Hôtel de la Place du Louvre
€€€€ **20 rooms**

Ⓜ *Pont-Neuf or Louvre-Rivoli. 21 rue des Prêtres-St-Germain-l'Auxerrois. 01 42 33 78 68. www.esprit-de-france.com. Breakfast 15€.*

This is an excellent address for lovers of the Louvre—it's only a minute's walk from the world-famous museum. It offers shipshape rooms, each named after a famous artist, and 5th floor duplexes. Some even have a view of the Louvre itself.

Hôtel Prince Albert Wagram
€€€€ **33 rooms**

Ⓜ *Villiers-Malesherbes. 28 passage Cardinet, access via 11 rue Jouffroy. 01 47 54 06 00. www.hotelprince albert.com. Breakfast 9€.*

Hidden in an alley, this recently renovated hotel just ten minutes by Métro to the Opéra district and the Arc de Triomphe offers practical rooms plus wifi.

MUST STAY

Hôtel de la Place du Louvre

Hôtel Powers
€€€€ **55 rooms**
Ⓜ *George-V or Alma-Marceau .*
52 rue François-1er. 01 47 23 91 05.
www.hotel-powers.com.
Breakfast 28€.
Discreet, pleasant hotel, just a
stone's throw from the world's
most celebrated avenue, the
Champs-Élysées. Spacious rooms
with period furnishings. some with
terraces and a view of the Eiffel
Tower. Sauna.

The Maison FL Hotel
€€€€ **61 rooms and 2 flats**
Ⓜ *Passy. 6 rue de La Tour. 01 55
74 75 75. www.maisonfl.com.*
Breakfast 20€.
An interesting 1930s building
located in the chic shopping
district with completely restored
Art Deco interior and comfortable,
spacious rooms, some with
balconies (from fifth floor up).

Millésime Hôtel
€€€€ **21 rooms**
Ⓜ *Saint-Germain-des-Prés.*
15 rue Jacob. 01 44 07 97 97.
www.millesimehotel.com.
Breakfast 16€.
This hotel in a 17C mansion right
in the heart of St-Germain des
Près has a spectacular (listed)
period staircase. The charming
Mediterranean courtyard is an
idea place to relax.

HOTELS

ARRONDISSEMENTS

Paris is divided into 20 districts or *arrondissements*.
Numbered from 1 to 20, the first is the most central district and from there the *arrondissements* are numbered consecutively, moving around the city in a clockwise spiral. Some areas straddle more than one *arrondissement*. The last one or two digits of Parisian zip/post codes beginning "75" indicate the *arrondissements*, e.g. 75006 = 6th *arrondissement*, 75018 = 18th *arrondissement*. *(See map on the inside back cover).* The list below details the *arrondissements* corresponding to areas mentioned in the guide.

1st Châtelet, Île de la Cité, Les Halles, Louvre, Palais-Royal, Tuileries

2nd Grands Boulevards, Les Halles, Place des Victoires

3rd Marais, République

4th Bastille, Beaubourg, Châtelet, Île-St-Louis, Marais

5th Jussieu, Latin Quarter, Maubert, Mouffetard

6th Latin Quarter, Montparnasse, Odéon, St-Germain-des-Prés, Sèvres-Babylone, St-Sulpice

7th Eiffel Tower, Faubourg St-Germain, Invalides

8th Champs-Élysées, Faubourg St-Honoré

9th Grands Boulevards, Opéra, Pigalle

10th Grands Boulevards, Canal St-Martin

11th Bastille, Belleville, Faubourg St-Antoine, République

12th Bastille, Bercy, Faubourg St-Antoine

13th Gobelins

14th Denfert-Rochereau, Montparnasse, Port-Royal

15th Montparnasse, Eiffel Tower

16th Auteil, Bois de Boulogne, Passy, Trocadéro

17th Champs-Élysées

18th Montmartre

19th Belleville, Canal St-Martin, Pigalle, La Villette

20th Belleville, Père-Lachaise

INDEX

PARIS

Churches, cinemas, clubs, galleries, markets, museums, parks and gardens, and theaters are listed under **bold headings**. For complete lists of hotels, restaurants, and shops, see the Must Do, Must Eat, and Must Stay sections.

INDEX

INDEX

p 82

©Michal Bednarek/Dreamstime.com

TABLE OF CONTENTS

5

★★★ ATTRACTIONS

Unmissable historic and cultural sights

Musée Condé, Château de Chantilly p 102

© Vidler Steve / age fotostock

Notre-Dame p 74

©Andre Pessoa / Fotolia.com

Église du Dôme p 73

© Y. Kanazawa / Michelin

Chartres Cathedral p 103

© J.J. Carton / Photoshot

MUST KNOW